Lynda

Dear Dawn,

Happy birthday.

Bless you!

Lynda 2012

Lynda

*From Accident & Trauma
to Healing & Wholeness!*

Lynda Scott

Sovereign World

Sovereign World Ltd
PO Box 784
Ellel
Lancaster LA1 9DA
England

www.sovereignworld.com

ISBN 978 1 85240 539 7

The publishers aim to produce books which will help to extend and build up the Kingdom of God. We do not necessarily agree with every view expressed by the authors, or with every interpretation of Scripture expressed. We expect readers to make their own judgment in the light of their understanding of God's Word and in an attitude of Christian love and fellowship.

Cover design by Andrew Mark, ThirteenFour Design
Cover & interior photography by Jonathan Dear, www.vibrantphotography.com.au
Typeset by Hurix
Printed in the United Kingdom

The Lord is my shepherd, I shall not be in want.
He makes me lie down in green pastures,
he leads me beside still waters,
he restores my soul.
He guides me in paths of righteous righteousness for his name's sake.
Even though I walk through the valley of the shadow of death,
I will fear no evil, for you are with me;
your rod and your staff, they comfort me.
You prepare a table before me in the presence of my enemies.
You anoint my head with oil; my cup overflows.
Surely goodness and love will follow me all the days of my life,
and I will dwell in the house of the Lord for ever.

Psalm 23

DEDICATION

I dedicate this book to those whom I love and are so precious to me, each of whom has walked a part of this journey with me. I could not have done it without any of you.

For my Heavenly Father and Jesus Christ, my most wonderful friend – You have shown Your love to me: this is for Your glory. I love You.

For Mum and Dad – you are both so amazing. Every step of the way you have been there for me. Thank you so much for all you have sacrificed for me. You are the best parents in the world. I honor you and love you.

For Inge Garvan – you have been the most faithful friend. You are a star.

For Peter Horrobin – I have been so blessed and humbled by your kindness, love and friendship. Thank you so much for believing in me and wanting me to write this book.

For my beautiful husband Leigh – you are the best earthly gift I have ever received. I love you with all my heart.

For Jack, Lily and Jasmyn – I dedicate this book to your memory, so that through it your destinies on this earth will be fulfilled. I look forward with all my heart to sharing eternity with you in heaven.

For Kirilee, Laura and Izaak – I write this book for you so that you may understand the legacy from which you have come and that as you grow, you will believe and learn to trust and love

Jesus, following Him and being faithful to Him until your last breath. This is my prayer for you. He will always be there for you. I love you so much.

I also want to dedicate this book to every person around the world who is a part of Ellel Ministries. Thank you for the amazing work you do.

CONTENTS

FOREWORD BY PETER HORROBIN

There are certain moments in all our lives which prove to be of great and lasting significance. For me, watching God heal Lynda was one of those moments which are indelibly printed on my memory. It was both unforgettable and life-changing, not only for Lynda, but for every single person present. When God healed Lynda, my faith and trust in Him rose to a new level of understanding. We had all watched a miracle take place.

But this wasn't a miracle that was a supernatural wonder performed by God without any human participation. The miracle was the culmination of a very courageous faith walk, during which Lynda had to face up to the reality of all she had gone through and deal with the real issues of forgiveness, and all the inner pain that had tormented her since she walked off a cliff into a rock-strewn ravine and fractured her spine in four places. It was a totally life-shattering accident – an accident that robbed her of life's opportunities, career fulfillment and even hope itself, especially the hope of marriage and family that is every girl's dream.

Lynda was existing in the twilight world of knowing that God loved her, but thinking, "What's the point of living when none of my dreams can ever be fulfilled and God hasn't answered my prayers?" Life had begun to lose its point. Suicidal thoughts were beginning to taunt her mind when, as a nurse, she attended a conference for Christian medical professionals organized by Health Care In Christ.

Those of us who were speaking at the conference were also facing our own issues as we stood before this large group of medical professionals. We wondered how they would respond to the teaching and stories we would tell about healing. We could only be true to the pilgrimage God had been taking us along since the work of Ellel Ministries had been established in 1986. This was an era when much of the Church was still extremely suspicious of many aspects of the healing ministry, especially deliverance – in spite of the words "deliver us from the evil one" being part of the Lord's Prayer, which most congregations still said at every service!

We had no idea how this specialist group of scientifically trained men and women would respond to the teaching which began with the simple statement that "healing is the restoration of godly order in every area of a person's life." We had seen, on many occasions, how when people choose to bring their lives into line with the truth about both God and man, God is always there to bring His blessing into their lives. We had regularly seen God transform people's lives when they chose to walk in His ways – including healing of long-term conditions.

In John 8:31 Jesus said that if we hold to His teaching – and that means apply it in our lives – then we really will be His disciples, and then we will know the truth and the truth will set us free. Many times I had heard people say to those in need, "The truth will set you free," without doing anything to help them walk in their healing and experience the freedom that Jesus promised. For the truth won't set people free if there are basic unresolved issues in their lives that are a blockage to their healing. Even Jesus had to say that if people didn't forgive others, His Father in heaven wouldn't be able to forgive them (Matthew 6:15).

When the day of Lynda's healing came she allowed God to show her all the things that had stood in the way of her recovery from the accident. She experienced deep inner healing through forgiveness. Not only had her body been physically injured and broken in the accident but she, herself, was broken on the inside. As God healed and delivered her she became progressively more free of all the hindrances to her healing until the time came when we anointed her with oil, as the disciples of Jesus had done

(Mark 6:13), and stood back to see what God would do. I won't spoil her story by telling you exactly what happened – this is Lynda's story, not mine. But her whole experience of what God did in her life that night is an amazing testimony to the grace and mercy of a loving God, who is still healing people today.

What God did was beyond the knowledge and experience of all the medics who were present. There was no need to argue the point that God heals today – they had seen it happen. As a result many lives, ministries and even medical practices were radically changed. The blind man said to those who challenged his healing, "One thing I do know. I was blind, but now I see!" (John 9:25). One thing Lynda, and everyone else knew, was that before the meeting she was disabled and in constant pain, but after the meeting her disability was gone. And her healing has not only stood the test of time but since that day Lynda has worked in some very tough and challenging environments.

God restored to her the hope and desire of her heart for a husband, marriage and family, but then she had to live through a series of devastating personal family traumas. This is no ordinary story. It challenges our thinking at the very deepest level and touches the heart in places that few other stories can reach.

I read the manuscript of this book on a flight, and was very aware of what other people might be thinking, as I was constantly having to wipe the tears from my eyes! The story of Lynda's pilgrimage through the dark nights of her own soul is one of the most moving passages of testimony I have ever read. This whole book is an incredible testimony to the triumphs of God's grace over the adversities that man can experience in what is so often a dangerous and hostile world. Her faith shines through from beginning to end – even through the times when the threads being sown into the tapestry of her life were all very dark in their color.

This book will be such an encouragement to those who are asking hard questions about the real issues of life and are looking for real answers. The answers Lynda found are there for all to see and experience for themselves. I pray that for many this book will prove to be their door of hope and the means through which they are able to lift their eyes beyond the obstacles of their life and know the healing love of God for themselves.

Peter Horrobin
Founder and International Director, Ellel Ministries International

For details of Ellel Ministries Centers worldwide, training courses and healing retreats, please go to ***www.ellelministries.org***

ACKNOWLEDGMENTS

There are so many people that I want to thank for their contribution towards the production of this book. Firstly I must give the biggest thanks to Peter Horrobin, the International Director of Ellel Ministries. Peter has held this book in vision for a number of years and obviously knew about it well before I ever did. It has been an absolute privilege to know Peter and his wife Fiona and I want to thank them both, and Ellel Ministries International, for giving me this opportunity to share my story in this book. I am really honored. Thank you, Peter, for sharing my story with so many people all over the world and allowing God to use it to help people understand His heart to heal victims of accidents and trauma. I would not have wanted anyone else but you, Peter, to write the Foreword, as you are the one person who has had such a heart for sharing my story. Thank you for the time you have given me in the midst of your busy schedule. You are amazing!

I want to thank the team at Sovereign World Ltd and my Publisher, Paul Stanier. Paul has been really wonderful and helped me work through the whole process of producing a book. Sandy Waldron, my editor, has also been fantastic and I want to thank her for the skill with which she has drawn the book together. Paul and Sandy, you have been a delight to work with – thank you so much.

In Chapter 6 there are a number of contributions from some of the dear people who were present the night I was healed. A big thankyou to Peter and Fiona Horrobin, Paul and Diane Watson, Dr Ken and Ros Curry, Dr Greg Foote and Drs Chris and Cate Hayes. What you have written has given the reader a glimpse of that amazing night we all shared together in 1996, that none of us will ever forget. Thank you for being a part of it, then and now.

The cover photograph and some of the other photographs for the book were taken by Jonathan Dear of Vibrant Photography. Thank you so much, Jonathan, for coming to spend the night with us and for doing the photo shoot on a very cold, windy winter day. You are a fantastic photographer. Thanks also to your wife Naomi for her support.

I would not have been able to have the time to write this book without the amazing support of my mum and dad. They have helped me with minding the children, so I could commit the time to write and have been the most invaluable support to me. Mum and Dad have seen me through the whole story, both mountains and valleys, and of everyone have been my greatest cheer squad. Thank you for standing with me, praying for me and always believing in me. This book is your story as well as mine.

Thank you so much to my husband Leigh and my children, Kirilee, Laura and Izaak. You have inspired me and encouraged me. I could not have done it without you.

I want to thank all those who have supported me in prayer throughout the production of the book. Thank you to my pastors, Jeff and Rowena Lloyd, and everyone at C3 Church Bathurst. Thank you to Inge Garvan for all her encouragement, and to Greg and Merle Foote, and Paul and Diane Watson for their prayer support at specific crucial times. I really appreciate everything you have done.

Finally I want to thank everybody who has been a part of this amazing story. Many I have mentioned, some I could not. But for whatever your contribution has been into my life, great or small, I want to bless you and thank you. The story would not have been the same without you.

INTRODUCTION

At age twenty-three I had everything going for me. I had recently completed a nursing diploma and was looking forward to a fulfilling career in my chosen profession. In the words of my mum I was "a happy, enthusiastic and competent young lady, full of life and throwing herself into all she put her hand to." I had grown up in a loving Christian family with parents who fully supported me. I had enjoyed a carefree childhood growing up, with my older sister Robyn and older brother Owen, on our parents' dairy farm in an idyllic corner of New South Wales in the south-east of Australia, in the tiny locality of White Rock. Down one side of our property there was a river and to the east were the Blue Mountains, which I loved to gaze at through my bedroom window. We were tucked away in our tiny slice of heaven.

Then a freak accident while on a Christian Mission Training School totally turned my life upside down. On a night hike I plunged down a thirty-five-foot cliff and my companions thought I must be dead. As well as suffering emotional and spiritual damage as a result of the accident, I suffered long-term physical effects. I had constant pain in my lower back which prevented me from undertaking anything but the lightest of tasks. I could only sit for short periods without the pain intensifying. Standing and lying down would bring momentary relief, but then the pain would soon come in those positions also. I constantly had to change my position, which was very difficult to cope with. I would have headaches at any time and debilitating attacks of vertigo. Some days the pain was worse than others. I would never know when I woke in the morning whether the pain would be bearable that day or completely incapacitating.

I became afraid of the pain, not wanting to push myself for fear of more pain. I was unable to commit to anything as I never knew if I would be able to maintain the commitment. My life revolved around the pain. There was nothing that doctors could do to help me.

I had come to faith in Jesus Christ when I was twelve years old through a Christian beach mission in the small coastal town of Queenscliff, Victoria, where our family went each Christmas holidays to visit my grandparents. Progressively since that time God had become my constant friend and companion. I had found it relatively easy to hear His voice as I came to know Him, but now, when I really needed His comfort and strength, my prayers seemed to bounce back at me from the roof and I felt very alone. Heaven seemed closed to me. Joy and hope were replaced by depression and despair. The prospect of living filled me with despair and I became suicidal.

To me at that time, and to most people hearing about what had happened to me, my situation seemed a disaster. It seemed that God had deserted me when I needed Him most and I was condemned to an existence that would be a mere shadow of the life I could have enjoyed. But this evaluation is far from the truth.

A year before the accident, early in 1993, I had been at a Vineyard conference in Sydney, the main speaker of which was Dr John White from Canada. I recall the evening so clearly. Mum, my brother Owen and I had just been to see the Geelong Cats, our football team, play against the Sydney Swans. Then, after the game, we all went over to the conference at Randwick Baptist Church, which was the church I was attending at that time. We were running a bit late and the church was very full, so we sat in the back row upstairs. I was still wearing my football jumper but tried to disguise it under another, tan-colored, woolen jumper. After Dr White's message he handed over to his own pastor who was traveling with him (I wish I had written down his name, but unfortunately I didn't). He wanted to give a prophetic word.

This is when God the Holy Spirit comes upon a person and they can speak a specific word to a person. Primarily these are words of encouragement, exhortation and edification. After first addressing another person, the pastor looked up to the back row and asked the young woman wearing the tan sweater to stand. I looked all around trying to find someone else that met the description, but, not finding anyone, concluded he must mean me! This had never happened to me before. I stood, my heart pounding. What he said to me was one of the most profound things I have ever heard. It was God the Father speaking directly to me and this is what He said: "I have heard the cry of your heart and I am going to show you how much I love you!"

This was one of the most pivotal moments in my life and everything that has happened to me since, I have realized, has come out of God my Father being faithful to this word. My heart's cry was to know God my Father, to please Him and love Him, and I was prepared to do whatever He asked of me. I was not sure what God was going to do with my life, but I trusted Him implicitly.

This trust has not led, as many Christians hope and imagine it will, to an easy life, crowned with success and material blessing, but to a life in which – as well as times of very real blessing – I have faced trauma, loss and deep heartache, first through the accident but, as you will discover in reading my story, through further trauma and heavy loss in my life. I went through a great struggle being single, wondering if God would ever bring the right spouse for me. Miraculously God did bring the right man for me and just as everything seemed to be going great, we were devastated by the loss of our first two children through late miscarriages. Yet through it God has shown me the priceless value of children, even though we were yet to face an even more devastating setback than we could have imagined. It has been my experience that as I have determined to trust the Lord, no matter what circumstances I find myself in, He has been able to work in my circumstances sometimes in a very dramatic way and then turn them around to His glory and through it bring me immeasurable joy.

I invite you to share my story of accident and trauma, and I trust you will be amazed, inspired and challenged as you see for yourself how God transformed my life with His healing and has miraculously brought me through to wholeness and fulfillment in a way only He could do.

Chapter 1

BROKEN

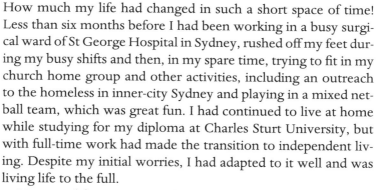

How much my life had changed in such a short space of time! Less than six months before I had been working in a busy surgical ward of St George Hospital in Sydney, rushed off my feet during my busy shifts and then, in my spare time, trying to fit in my church home group and other activities, including an outreach to the homeless in inner-city Sydney and playing in a mixed netball team, which was great fun. I had continued to live at home while studying for my diploma at Charles Sturt University, but with full-time work had made the transition to independent living. Despite my initial worries, I had adapted to it well and was living life to the full.

Now my life was quite a different story. I had taken a break from nursing to do the Mission Training School and to give myself time to explore what direction God was wanting me to take in my life, but the accident had thrown me into a no-man's land. I wanted to be able to work but I just couldn't manage it. Nursing is a very physically demanding job and I was still having serious trouble with gnawing pain in my lower back, poor concentration and, most of all, constant fatigue. The headaches were still an almost-daily occurrence and attacks of vertigo were still forcing me to spend whole days in bed. Physically I was very limited. I could only walk short distances and I really struggled going up a flight of stairs. I was eligible for a welfare benefit, called Sickness Benefits, and although it was not much money, I lived simply and it kept me going.

My life seemed to revolve around getting to hospital appointments, of which there were about three a week at first. After the initial follow-up appointments subsequent to the accident I had been left very much to my own devices, but, as time wore on and my condition was not improving, I went back to my GP and started getting referred to different services that I hoped might be able to help me. For a short time I had physiotherapy, and as part of that I went to the Hydrotherapy Pool at the local hospital. All I could manage was to float in a rubber tube in the pool. I recalled how I had been the swimming champion in high school and here I was floating in a rubber tube. I felt so useless.

I did start to study to keep my mind active, commencing a Graduate Certificate in Women's Health Nursing. The study was supposed to be for eight hours per week and I could do it from home. It was good to think about something new and I enjoyed it. Despite struggling to keep up, needing extensions to complete my work, I did stick to it and received really good marks, which was encouraging.

For a while I lived with some girls who were connected to the Mission Training School, but after a couple of months I moved in with a lovely friend of mine and her parents, who were very kind and supportive. Nevertheless, as time went on, I became more and more isolated and lonely. Everyone else had their lives to get on with. The process of rehabilitation was far from easy and while I was extremely grateful for all that the doctors and medical professionals were trying to do for me, the knowledge was gradually dawning on me that they were running out of options.

Emotionally and spiritually, as well as physically, it was a very hard time for me. I was amazed at the effect pain has on you. It is so draining. I was angry, too, that it should affect my relationship with God. But it did. I wanted to be close to God, but He seemed a long way away. Gradually I came to accept that I had become depressed and went to see a doctor about it. From my own immature perspective before the accident, I thought that a Christian should never be depressed. But I knew I loved God, I was a Christian and

I was depressed. I did not want it to be like that, but in being real with myself as I sought to be, I knew it was so. Thankfully I had the humility to admit it and I started taking antidepressant medication. The issue for me was really one of hope. I needed something to hope for that was good, but hope seemed to be draining out my toes. It got to the point where I was not living from day to day or week to week any more, but from minute to minute. I even considered suicide, just to end the pain. I could feel at times a tangible sense of "brokenness." All the parts inside of me were broken.

I recalled an incident at the beginning of that year, before the Mission Training School, where God had spoken to me and asked me if I would trust Him with my life, even if it included physical suffering. I had told God I would trust Him. But in the midst of the suffering I was now enduring, I was ashamed of my own weakness. If only I could trust Him more.

There were a few things that God used to help me through that difficult time. One was the support of my few remaining friends in Sydney, especially my best friend Inge, from high school days, who came to spend time with me and was deeply concerned at my state of mind. I kept in regular communication with Mum and Dad and knew they were praying for me. I also used to get beautiful letters from a dear old lady named Peg, whom I knew from my home church in Bathurst, the closest town to White Rock. God must have put me on her heart because she would write me a note to encourage me and tell me she was still praying for me. At one very critical point I remember I had a phone call from an old friend whom I had not heard from for a long time and it was enough to give me hope and see me through some dark days. Sometimes it is just those seemingly small and insignificant kindnesses that can make the difference between life and death.

At Christmas I returned home for the holidays. One day, as I was sitting by my bedroom window thinking and praying, I heard the sweet sound of God's voice again: "Why don't you come home?" The thought of it gave me a surge of hope. So at the beginning of 1995 I moved home again. What a year it had been! I had been through the mincing machine. I was now in a place where I could receive some tender loving care that only a family can give.

Chapter 2

A Divine Appointment

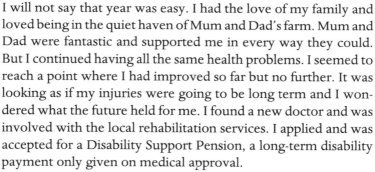

I will not say that year was easy. I had the love of my family and loved being in the quiet haven of Mum and Dad's farm. Mum and Dad were fantastic and supported me in every way they could. But I continued having all the same health problems. I seemed to reach a point where I had improved so far but no further. It was looking as if my injuries were going to be long term and I wondered what the future held for me. I found a new doctor and was involved with the local rehabilitation services. I applied and was accepted for a Disability Support Pension, a long-term disability payment only given on medical approval.

The direction God took me when I returned to Bathurst was to engage in creative pursuits. I started doing pottery one or two nights a week, as I could manage it. Without even realizing it, as I was creating things God was restoring my soul and healing my spirit. I also did a sewing course and started making some of my own clothes. This met a similar need in me. I really enjoyed creating and it made me feel good.

I continued to do my nursing studies at about half the pace that I had started it. Through it I undertook a major assignment on Natural Family Planning, which God used to lead me to a local doctor, Anne Gilroy, who was the consultant for Natural Family Planning in the area. I went to meet with Anne and it was like a divine appointment.

25

Anne was a Christian and had not long started her own General Practice. In the course of our conversation I told her about the accident and that I had not been able to work. We talked about an organization called Health Care In Christ (HCIC), which I had been involved with initially when I was at St George Hospital in Sydney. It is a group of Christian health professionals across Australia to whom God gave the vision and passion to be witnesses for Him in their workplaces. The strategy that God gave them was for Christian health workers to go out two by two. Anne had heard of Health Care In Christ and was really wanting to see her own practice and, more broadly, the whole health service of Bathurst impacted by the love and healing of Jesus. Anne and I just clicked that day and by the time I was leaving she had offered me a part-time job to work as her practice nurse! It was so amazing.

So in September 1995 I started doing five hours per week as Anne's practice nurse. It was a really big step for me and I was so thankful to Anne for her kindness in working with my disability and giving me the freedom to work at my own pace. In the following weeks we built the hours up to ten hours per week – two blocks of five hours. That was all I could manage. The fatigue I had experienced since the accident just went on and on. No matter how much sleep I got, I was always tired. Ten hours of work became my limit and I could not manage more. But I was so grateful to be working and the depression and despair I had felt the previous year had now gone.

There were times even into 1996 when the vertigo would return and make me very ill. I would wake in the middle of the night feeling as if the bed was rotating off the floor. All I could do was wait until it settled again over a number of days before I could resume my normal activities. In May of 1996 I had four weeks of severe abdominal pain and nausea. I was admitted to hospital for a week and found to have multiple small stomach ulcers, as a result of the medication I had been taking for the back pain. That was a setback. I wondered if this suffering was ever going to end. I went through some treatment for the ulcers, which did not work, so I started a new course of treatment. There was a HCIC conference coming up, and I had decided that, whatever the next conference was about, I was going to it. No matter how bad my health was, I was going to be there.

That year's Health Care In Christ Conference was on the theme of "Evangelism, Healing and Deliverance." It was a four-day conference and was being held at the beautiful Merroo Conference Center on the western outskirts of Sydney. There were about 150 delegates attending the conference, primarily doctors, allied health professionals and pastors.

The main speakers were Peter and Fiona Horrobin of Ellel Ministries in England, with one of their directors Jill Southern also teaching at some of the sessions. Before the conference I remember so clearly thinking that the topic seemed a bit "odd." I had never heard anyone teach on these three subjects together and I wondered what we were going to be in for. On arrival, full of anticipation, I settled into my room and made friends with my room-mate, a lovely lady named Diane Watson.

The first two days of the conference were amazing. Peter was teaching on the foundations of the Christian faith. I was totally gripped. Even though I had been a Christian for a long time, I had never heard anyone teach with such clarity and explain so many of the fundamental questions that people have about the Christian faith. He taught on the Fall of the human race in the Garden of Eden and how man gave his rightful power and authority to Satan. To reclaim that authority was one of the main reasons why Jesus had to come. Having explained the foundations, Peter went on to teach about the healing ministry of Jesus. Looking at the New Testament again I realized that evangelism, healing and deliverance was the everyday ministry of Jesus! I had really only learned about evangelism – I knew very little about healing and nothing about deliverance. Peter also taught thoroughly on the subject of deliverance, addressing the common misconception that Christians cannot have demons. He clearly taught that Christians can have demons, but not be possessed by them, and the wonderful news is that through Jesus we can be set free (or delivered) from them.

Physically I struggled during the conference. Sitting for long periods really hurt my back and I was extremely fatigued, but the teaching was so gripping that I pushed through my physical discomfort, because I did not want to miss anything.

On the third day, Peter and Fiona started to teach about bringing healing to people who had been victims of accident or major trauma. Since the beginning of Ellel ten years previously in 1986, Jesus had revealed to them some important keys about how to pray for people who had been in serious accidents. They shared a number of amazing stories of how God had brought healing to people they had prayed for all around the world. The very basic principle of their teaching on receiving healing from accident and trauma is that as humans we are three-part beings, made up of spirit, soul and body (1 Thessalonians 5:23b). When a person is in an accident, the body receives all the attention, while the broken soul and spirit are given little or no attention. Another common consequence of an accident is that a person can get demonized because of the massive shock and trauma suffered, with Satan taking advantage of the person in their weak and defenseless state. This obviously compounds his or her problems. As a result of this brokenness, many people never regain their pre-accident health. This was me! I sat there shaking.

In the afternoon tea-break I told Diane about the accident I had suffered and she went to get Fiona Horrobin. As Fiona and Diane listened, I poured out my story.

Chapter 3

THE ACCIDENT

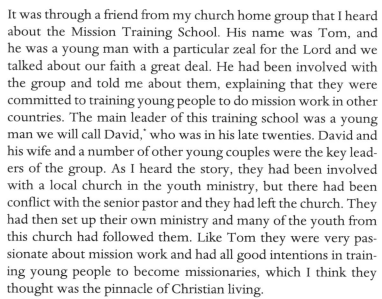

It was through a friend from my church home group that I heard about the Mission Training School. His name was Tom, and he was a young man with a particular zeal for the Lord and we talked about our faith a great deal. He had been involved with the group and told me about them, explaining that they were committed to training young people to do mission work in other countries. The main leader of this training school was a young man we will call David,* who was in his late twenties. David and his wife and a number of other young couples were the key leaders of the group. As I heard the story, they had been involved with a local church in the youth ministry, but there had been conflict with the senior pastor and they had left the church. They had then set up their own ministry and many of the youth from this church had followed them. Like Tom they were very passionate about mission work and had all good intentions in training young people to become missionaries, which I think they thought was the pinnacle of Christian living.

The structure that they put together to achieve their training goals was to run training schools. Over the summer holidays

---

* All the names in this account of the accident have been changed to protect identity.

they ran a two-month training school for university students and
I attended some of the activities on my days off. During one of
those visits David approached me and invited me to consider
signing up for an upcoming Missions Training School (MTS)
starting in March 1994. I think the thing that appealed to me
was the number of other young people involved, all of whom
were very passionate about the Lord. I was open to the idea of
mission work, but God had not given me any specific leading
that He wanted me to be a missionary. The course was to run
for sixteen weeks full time. Learning more about God and studying the Bible more closely with other young people, I thought
sounded great, so I decided to sign up. I resigned from my full-
time nursing position and got ready to start the MTS. Mum and
Dad were not really keen on me doing it, but they understood
my motives and respected my decision. They felt a little uneasy
with David, whom they'd met once when they'd come with me
to have a look at the training center soon after I'd enrolled. At
the beginning of the course, they dropped me off at the training
school en route to the airport as Mum was going on a six-week
holiday to Israel and the United Kingdom.

There were six students enrolled in our school. I was the old-
est at twenty-three. The two other girls were Sarah and Ali, both
a few years younger than me. We shared a cabin together on the
compound and became friends. The three young men's names
were Mike, Josh and Sam. They had not long finished school
and were maybe eighteen or nineteen years old. David and his
wife were the main leaders and teachers of the material at the
school. They lived at the training center along with a few other
couples and a few single people who were also involved in the
training. Their input was supplemented by others who would
visit the training school to bring teaching. They were a part of
the broader leadership of the group. One of these leaders we will
call John.

Implicit within the MTS was our acceptance of the leaders'
authority and the understanding that our actions were to be
based on complete submission. We did not have any right to
question what we were asked to undertake. We had to obey

and trust the leaders' judgment in everything. I had no reason to question this premise and like the other students just accepted that this was how things were.

As a part of the MTS the leaders established a series of "Faith Trips" for us. These were usually held on the weekend, to supplement our theoretical biblical learning. They were intended to take us out of our comfort zone and to make us trust God. The leaders also wanted us to learn to work together as a team and to help each other. The rationale for this was to prepare us for possible scenarios we might face if we were in a foreign country doing mission work.

We had been told to expect physical Faith Trips and so before the course started I purchased my first-ever pair of hiking boots and a fully supported hiking backpack. I had always enjoyed sports and physical activities at school, but I had never been hiking and was not physically prepared for such an activity. The first Faith Trip was a hike. We drove to a national park together and, with David leading us, we had to hike up a mountain. Some people love this sort of thing. I really struggled. It was very dense bush land with lots of trees and lots of rocks. It was very steep in parts. Covering such uneven ground with the pressure to keep up with the others was really difficult. I remember my legs shaking as I pushed myself to keep up. That night for the first time in my life I literally slept under a tree. Having grown up on a farm, I had always been conscious of the possibility of snakes and sleeping in the open like this caused me great internal anxiety. I stuffed it down, praying God would keep me safe. But I was scared.

David was aware that I was struggling with the hike. In the end he changed his original plan of a two-night hike to make it only the one night. I was so relieved, but at the same time I felt guilty and ashamed that I was not good enough and the hike had been cut short because of me.

At the end of March we all drove north to a farm owned by David's wife's parents, where we were to camp for eight to nine days to spend time seeking God. It was much more like the farm land I had come from and I felt comfortable there. We each had our own tent and we were given our own camping spot, each separate from the others. We had to construct our own tent and make our own campfire, meeting together once a day for a shared meal. I was camped by a small creek and I had a lovely time sitting by it and listening to the sweet sound of the flowing water. One morning as I slept in my tent some cows came and pushed on the ropes. I loved it there and felt really close to God.

On the 5th of April, late in the afternoon I was in my tent alone when I felt the presence of the Holy Spirit come tangibly upon my body. I was lying in my sleeping bag and felt a strong tingling sensation first on my head and then for about an hour moving all over my body. I did not feel Him move on my chest. I could sense/feel a breastplate covering it. This is the only time in my life I have had a tangible sense of the "breastplate of righteousness" referred to in Ephesians 6:14b. After some time, out of absolute curiosity I asked God what He was doing. I immediately heard a few quiet words in reply: "I am strengthening your body." I had no idea why He should need to do this, but I gave my full cooperation and asked Him to do whatever He needed to do. I recorded it in my diary and told David about it at the next community meal.

Following our return from the farm we continued our regular training. Our next Faith Trip was scheduled for Friday 15 April. This was to be another physical challenge. At the drop-off point David gave us our instructions: we were to walk down a path known as Bob Turners Track, which Mike in our group was familiar with; near a spot known to Mike we had to build bush huts out of branches and make camp for the night; then in the morning we were to hike along a ravine by the Colo River as far as we could go, making sure we were back at the drop-off point by 3 pm on Sunday afternoon. So Sarah, Ali, Mike, Josh, Sam and I set off down Bob Turners Track. Mike showed us where we were to camp. Sarah, Ali and I constructed one bush hut and the boys constructed another. We built a fire and ate some tinned food that we had brought with us. Sarah, Ali and I zipped our sleeping bags together for safety and warmth, and that night I slept on my back on the left side and did not move the whole night. I looked up at the leaves and branches over our heads and thought how this was the first time I had ever slept in a bush hut.

The next morning we had our breakfast, put on our hiking boots and backpacks, and set off along the course of the river. The ravine was in the shape of a V with the river flowing down the middle and two hills rising up either side. It was again fairly dense bush land with lots of tall, spindly gum trees and numerous rocks. The river was fairly deep in parts, but there were places where it was shallow enough for us to cross. It was completely isolated and felt a very lonely place. Mike took the lead and we all followed along one after the other.

Around lunchtime, after we had been walking for about four and a half hours, we were getting ready to stop for lunch and a short rest when from somewhere in the bushes on the other side of the ravine we heard John's voice calling out to us. If I remember correctly he called to us to "make camp." Mike, who had been involved with previous training schools, chose that moment to tell us how on other faith trips he had been on the leaders had actually ambushed the group. The thought that the leaders – and we didn't know how many – had been following us made us all a bit anxious. We half-expected them to leap out on us at any moment. I had had little to do with John up to that point. He had been at the training school a few times to teach, but I did not know him and did not know what to expect of him. The boys had a few army-style hutchies* in their packs, so they set them up in the trees. It was also starting to drizzle at this point. I would say we were all feeling a bit jumpy, thinking we might be attacked at any moment. We sat and waited, but nothing happened.

After hanging around for several hours not knowing what to expect, at around 5.00 pm we prepared our dinner over the campfire. We had been given an allowance to buy food and

---

* These are tents made out of waterproof sheeting that can be tied between trees with ropes.

somebody had bought some rice which we were going to cook in our billy. To give it more flavor the person cooking added the spice turmeric, common in Indian food, which made it yellow. I had not been accustomed to spices like that in my growing up and I can still remember the smell of the turmeric and rice as we ate it for dinner. It was awful, but it was food and all we had, so we ate it.

About 6 pm, as we were finishing our dinner, David, John and a young man named Tim walked into the camp. Tim, who was probably about twenty-one, lived at the MTS with us and helped out with different things, such as leading worship with his guitar. He was what I would have considered a leader in training. But David and John were the ones in charge. They both looked very angry and maybe disappointed too. David spoke first, rebuking us for the way we had handled the afternoon. He said we had failed to follow our instructions by erecting the hutchies and that we had used the time in a non-constructive manner. I can't speak for everyone else, but I felt like a little child caught red-handed doing something that made her father angry. We all looked at the ground feeling terrible.

After a while David and John stepped aside to speak privately. When they returned they told us they had a challenge for us, and David went around everyone asking, "Are you in?" I did not like the sound of this. We were not told what it was we were going to have to do. The question was ridiculous really, because we had absolutely no choice in the outcome – we had to do whatever we were told. David then announced that we were going to pack up the camp and hike back to the bush huts where we had camped the night before! The hike had taken us four and a half hours in daylight and we were going to be retracing our steps at 7 pm in the evening. It was already dark and, to make matters worse, the conditions had deteriorated significantly during the afternoon with the onset of light rain, which was going to make everything slippery and greasy. David told us we were all going to walk together and share our torches, but not take as many precautions as the six of us had taken that morning. I was absolutely paralyzed with fear. It was the only time in my whole life that I have been totally incapacitated by fear, to the point that I could not speak. I was still carrying the memory of the stress of the previous hike in the back of my mind and the prospect of what I was about to undertake completely terrified me. I knew also that I did not have a choice and that somehow I just had to do it. It was my worst nightmare. But I pushed the fear and terror down and tried to act as normally as I could.

The hike commenced. There were nine of us altogether. David led the way, demanding a much faster pace than we had walked on the way there. Before long he had us walking up the middle of the river. I had my own torch, but since not everyone else had one with an adequate battery, it was taken away from me and passed up the line to someone who needed it more. I think there were only about four working torches between the nine of us. I quickly fell to the back of the line. For the most part John and Tim were behind me, but they afforded me little help. My feet kept slipping on the rocks near the river, exacerbated by the lack of light. I was doing all I could just to keep going and to keep up. I did not want to end up feeling like I had after the first hike – full of guilt and shame. I heard the sounds of the water bubbling by, our feet sloshing through the river or tramping through the undergrowth, the whipping of prickly vines across our legs and the murmur of talking as we followed David along the river. The rain continued to fall lightly.

I was completely shut down inside. I had never felt like this before and I had no idea how to handle it. I prayed and asked God to help me. Each step was a step of faith. No one else seemed bothered that I could tell, or maybe they were putting on a brave face like I was – a mask to cover the fear.

Having crossed into the river a number of times, leeches in the river were latching onto my lower legs. I had never come across leeches before. They were disgusting. As well as thick socks under my hiking boots, I was wearing two pairs of long pants – one pair of blue-and-white-striped cotton pants and my favorite Geelong Football Club track pants – but these leeches got through everything. We stopped from time to time for a brief break and had to extract these leeches from our legs. It was at moments like these that I thought this hike was like walking through hell. I could not wait for it to be over.

After we had been hiking for some time, continuing along the river bank, somehow the group got broken up. Someone said we weren't far away from the bush huts where we were going to camp for the night. I felt a surge of relief that this nightmare might nearly be over.

David, being the fastest, was still out the front with Sarah and Ali. John and Tim had been behind me, but when I looked back they were gone. I had no idea where they went. I was now bringing up the rear behind Mike, Josh and Sam. Josh had my torch. I recall we approached a rock face jutting out over the river and to get past it we had to edge our way along a very narrow ledge. It looked very dangerous and I didn't know how I would get across. I could not work out where the other leaders had got to and could not believe that they would have us walk across this narrow ledge. Somehow we got past the ledge and started making our way upwards, which was the only way we could go. A feeling of terror started to rise within me. I told the guys I was worried and wanted to know where the leaders were. Being young 18-19-year-old men they were relishing the adventure and were not concerned by the leaders' absence. I looked out across the ravine and, far below us, I saw the beam from a torch coming across towards us. Although I felt relief to know there was someone there, it made me realize how high up in the ravine we were. Sam was in front of me and by this point he was helping me through every step.

By now we were in very dense bush land. I followed Mike, Josh and Sam as we all made our way carefully through the trees, trying to find the safest places for our feet. With only one torch up front with Josh, I was holding onto the trees for balance and stepping very warily. I very carefully extended my left foot across onto the ground which Sam had just vacated. Thinking I had my balance I let go of the tree. With greasy, wet boots and damp, slippery ground from the rain, my foot slipped and I lost my balance. I threw my left hand backwards to try to catch Sam. In that half a second as I started to fall I thought, "I have missed Sam" and then "I am going to fall into the river." At that moment I blacked out near the top of the cliff.

I awoke to the sounds of yelling and shouting and lights flashing all over the place. I was lying on my right side looking across the ground, trying to make sense of the scene. John was with me and he told me that I had fallen from a cliff, 30–35 feet. He had already cut off my backpack. It all felt so surreal. I had not fallen into the river as I had expected, but onto a dry creek bed and landed in some rocks. Mike, Josh and Sam had seen me fall. They told me I landed on my right side and then bounced forward landing face down, unmoving. They shone the torch on me and, seeing blood all around my head, they thought I was dead.

I was unconscious for maybe two minutes, John told me. It was now approximately 10.30 pm. On awaking I witnessed a scene of complete chaos. John and Tim were with me. Mike, Josh and Sam were stuck up on the cliff edge, thinking I was dead and unable, out of complete shock, to manage their way down. They were all yelling to David who was with Sarah and Ali, telling him I had fallen and they should go and get paramedic help. As it was told to me, David told Sarah, being the more physically fit of the two, that she was to hike out of the ravine with him to go and get some paramedics. He then turned to Ali and told her to make her way very carefully back to the rest of the group and wait there. The only problem was that Ali did not have a torch and David, in the confusion and panic, did not think to let anyone know that she was there. So dear Ali got down on her hands and knees and crawled up the ravine in the pitch black so she would not fall in the river. She stopped by a big rock and waited. David and Sarah went for help.

At the bottom of the cliff I was going through hell. I was trying to think like a nurse, but, in the midst of the shock and trauma, I could not. I had hit my head and there was blood all over the place. I had pain all over my body. I vomited a number of times and there was that rice and turmeric all over again. John took charge and decided not to move me in case I had a spinal injury.

So I remained lying on my right side in the rocks for a number of hours. John, who for the duration of the hike had hardly spoken to me, told me that for that night he was going to be my best friend. Anything I needed or wanted, I should just ask. I remember replying that it was better to have him as my friend for one night than not at all. He monitored my condition as best he could and kept a record of my pulse, writing it with match ash as he did not have a pen.

Very slowly Mike, Josh and Sam managed to make their way down the cliff and when they reached us, John had them build a fire. I remember them telling me later that Josh was in such a state of shock that he could not do a thing but sit, while Mike and Sam ripped down trees and built the biggest fire you have ever seen. Shock in the face of trauma affects everyone so differently. They did not build the fire too close to me, in case the smoke made me sick, but they wanted a fire to signal to the rescue team where we were.

John and Tim sat with me and were wonderful. Apart from the obvious pain and trauma I was strangely at peace. I asked Tim if he would sing for me some of the songs he sang in our worship times. He had a lovely voice and his singing brought great comfort to my spirit and soul. John offered to read to me from the Bible and asked me what my favorite passage was. It was hard to think of one, because I love all the passages in the Bible. Then I thought I would love to hear Psalm 23 – "The Lord is my Shepherd." So John read it to me and it was beautiful. I was literally in the "valley of the shadow of death" (verse 4) and I truly was not afraid there. Even though I had been so afraid during the hike, fear was not in my consciousness as I lay in the rocks waiting for the paramedics. I did not think of death or dying once throughout that whole night! It was in the forefront of everyone else's mind, but somehow God buffeted me from it and I only thought of living.

David returned with the paramedics after four and a half hours, now the middle of the night. My system was going into shock and I urgently needed some intravenous fluids to keep me alive. Needing to assess my injuries, the paramedics cut off nearly all my clothes, including my boots. I understood they needed to, but I still felt embarrassed. It was then I really felt the absence of any other women. Exhausted after hiking out to get the paramedics with David, Sarah had understandably not returned. It was then that it became apparent that Ali was nowhere to be found. Pandemonium struck again as it dawned on everyone that Ali was missing somewhere out in the ravine – all alone and with no torch. Emergency search teams and police were summoned by radio and a full-scale search commenced looking for her.

Once the paramedics arrived I felt really alone. Everyone was processing their own shock, as well as helping in the search for Ali. I was left lying in the paramedic tray, wishing someone would talk to me. As the night wore on, the physical pain I was feeling was intensifying, but because I had suffered a head injury the paramedics could not give me any pain-relieving medication. So the pain got really bad. I remember the paramedic asking me at one point to get my right arm out of the sleeping bag so he could take my blood pressure. It was excruciating to move my arm. Watching me struggle, he called me a "whinger," someone who was complaining. I was so hurt. It had not even crossed my mind that my elbow was broken, which it later proved to be.

By daylight Ali had still not been found and the search intensified. At about 9 am Sunday 17 April the rescue helicopter could be heard purring in the sky overhead and a paramedic winched me up into the helicopter. The sound of it made my already throbbing head throb some more. After ten and a half hours lying at the bottom of the cliff, I was finally off to hospital. By the grace of God I had survived.

Seeing and hearing the helicopter, Ali walked into the search camp, having spent the whole night next to a rock.

Chapter 4

WALKING THROUGH THE VALLEY

As the helicopter buzzed through the sky towards the hospital, I felt an overwhelming sense of relief. The nightmare was over. I'm going to be OK, I thought. The paramedic in the helicopter warned me that there might be some news crews waiting at the hospital, and there they were as I was wheeled into the Emergency Department. The story made the headlines on the national news that evening. In one report the police made a very unfavorable comment about a group with such inexperienced bushwalkers having been hiking in such terrible conditions.

As the doctors assessed my injuries and stabilized my condition, I felt an overwhelming feeling of exhaustion. I had not slept for maybe twenty-eight hours by then and all I wanted to do was sleep. I had a large laceration on the right side of my forehead that needed suturing, but as soon as the doctor put the sterile drape over my face to begin I fell straight asleep. I was so relieved to finally be able to sleep that I missed the whole procedure.

Later that day I was transferred to the neurosurgery high dependency. I awoke from my sleep to see Dad, my sister Robyn, her two daughters Bethany and Katrina, and my Aunty Mavis walking through the door. (My brother Owen had stayed home to record all the new reports on the television!) Aunty Mavis was crying. Maybe if I had looked in the mirror I would have cried too. I called out to Bethany, who was three and a half at the time, telling her to come over to me, but she stared at me with the most puzzled look on her face. She wanted further proof that I was really Aunty Lynda, because I looked nothing like me. The blow to my head had given me a massive black eye, causing my right eye to close, and as the day went on it extended over my nose into my left eye. I looked like I had been in a boxing match. My head was covered in bandages and the hair poking out had gone pink from all the blood. Bethany was smart enough to know that this lady lying in the hospital bed wearing a white hospital gown did not look like Aunty Lynda, even though she might have sounded roughly the same.

Dad told me about an experience he had had the night before. He had been asleep in bed when at about 10.30 pm he had woken up bolt upright in bed and heard me calling him! Not knowing what to do he went back to bed. At about 5 am, having got up to go to the bathroom, he saw a police car coming up the driveway. It was a courtesy visit to tell him that I had been in an accident. They did not have many details. Dad asked if I was still alive, and they said I was. At that moment God gave Dad a supernatural gift of faith and he knew that I was going to be all right. As Dad visited me that first day in the hospital there was a strength in him that I had never seen before. He seemed to rise to the occasion, becoming strong at a time when I was totally weak.

Over the course of the next week a diagnosis of my injuries was gradually made. I had a massive soft tissue injury to the right side of my lower back, which had taken the major impact of the fall, despite having been cushioned to some degree by my backpack with my sleeping bag. The force was so great that the right transverse processes had fractured from L2 to L5, with the tips of L4 and L5 completely detaching from the spine. That meant that the blow to my right lower back was huge. When after a few days I managed, with the help of a nurse, to get out of bed and get wheeled into the shower, I remember looking at my back in the mirror for the first time. It was scary. The swelling took my back out maybe 20–30 cm! I had never seen anything like it, even in my nursing experience. In the middle of the bruising there was a part that went completely grey. It was probably the center of the impact. I suffered total numbness in that area as a result of nerve damage, and even after the bruising subsided that numbness remained in my back for months and months.

The next most significant impact was taken by my head, which hit the rocks and bounced off before hitting the rocks again. As well as the big gash to my forehead, which the doctor had stitched up, I had two fractures to my skull around my right eye – hence my two black eyes. I was also diagnosed with a mild brain injury. I underwent initial assessment for this in the hospital, but had to have a range of continuing assessments and follow-up. It was the head injury that caused the severe vertigo, making my head just start to spin. This was very difficult to manage – especially as it could happen anywhere and at any time – and something that the doctors could not do very much about. They said it would "settle in time."

I had a lot of pain in my right shoulder and neck, where the impact had also been taken, but no fractures. I also had the most massive bruise on my right thigh. How some of these other bones did not break could only be attributable to God having supernaturally strengthened my body the week before the accident. I also noted that where God showed me the "breastplate of righteousness" was, I had no injuries. A thought that never really occurred to me at the time but has since is that I could have ended up a paraplegic or even a quadriplegic – so great was the trauma my body experienced! My right elbow was broken – I had chipped the end off the bone. Hearing that, I understood why it had hurt so much to try to move my right arm out to have my blood pressure taken at the bottom of the cliff. The last fracture was my middle finger on my left hand.

I had gone through massive trauma, but truly amazingly they could not do anything for any of the fractured bones. The back fractures just had to heal themselves, as did the fractures around my eye. The elbow, being a chip fracture, only required a dressing to keep it clean. The fracture to my finger needed a small finger splint. The brain injury, the vertigo and the bruising would, the doctors said, all heal in time.

I had quite a lot of visitors in hospital, but that didn't stop me missing Mum. She was the person I would have wanted to have with me the most. It was so awful to be going through all of this without her. I so wished she was there. Dad had decided not to tell her the extent of my injuries so she could finish her holiday, which was the first big holiday of her life. He told her that I had had a "bit of an accident" and was in hospital, but I was OK. When she received his call, Mum was in a small town called Strathpeffer in the north of Scotland. As women often do, Mum knew Dad was not telling her the whole story. She went into a beautiful church there and prayed to our Father in heaven, knowing He could be with me. Mum trusted Him to look after me, which He did.

That first week I went through a whole mixture of feelings. Emotionally I went through feelings of having failed at the hike when I had tried so hard, going through the same feelings of guilt and shame as I had felt after the first hike. I also felt guilty for putting everyone, especially the other students, through such a traumatic night. Ali could also have been injured, or worse, in the panic of the events. I was really glad it had not been me crawling in pitch black on my hands and knees through that ravine and sleeping alone next to a rock. The other person I really felt for was Sam. He had thrown out his hand and tried to save me from falling. I was concerned at the guilt that he would be feeling, thinking he had "dropped me."

David had come to see me at the hospital, along with a few of the other leaders. He apologized to me and said that he and John should never have taken us on that hike. He told me that I should not worry about any medical expenses or the like, assuring me that they would provide what I needed.

I was discharged from the hospital six days after the accident, carrying a lot of pain, but hope for the future. I did not know what lay ahead of me. It was my first admission as a patient and I had rarely ever gone to a doctor. I was positive about the future, believing everything would be OK and believing David's promise that they would provide for me. So with these thoughts in mind I chose to return to MTS. I did not entertain any other option. I am by nature a very wholehearted person and if I take something on, I finish it. I went back to try and make sense out of what had just happened.

Sometimes in life I have found that you have a moment where all you have just been through crystallizes. I had such a moment when I got back to my room at the Missions Training School and saw my hiking boots. I had only bought them a month before and, seeing the state they were in now, everything I had been through the previous week hit me like a ton of bricks. They were in the most terrible state. The laces were in shreds where John had cut through them with his pocket-knife after I had fallen. The leather was battered, as a result of the terrain we had walked through, and misshapen, having dried out after being saturated with water. They had scratch marks all over them. Although I was trying to put a brave face on it, that was how I was feeling on the inside. How I had survived was only by the amazing saving power and grace of God.

The early weeks of my return to MTS were hard. I had constant back pain and headaches. Some days all I could do was get out of bed and have a shower before feeling so exhausted that I would have to go back to bed and sleep. In those early weeks the vertigo was really severe. If the vertigo came on while I was lying in bed, my head would spin and I would feel as if the bed was rotating like helicopter blades. I would just hold on to the bed, so I did not fall off. It was very scary. Sometimes I got the vertigo in the shower when I put my head back to wash my hair and then I would nearly fall. It also meant that I could not drive, which meant I became completely dependent on others to get me around. That was really hard.

Emotionally it was hard for all of us. Ali had been left alone in the ravine for the whole night. Mike, Josh and Sam had seen me fall and had thought I was dead! We all talked through what had happened at length, each trying to process the trauma of that night. They all really wanted to help me in any way they could. David seemed a bit detached emotionally. I never really had any idea what he thought or felt about my situation. A few weeks after the accident John came to do some teaching and I could see his feelings written all over his face. He was so sorry and in such

obvious turmoil that I could only imagine that guilt was tortur-
ing him inside. It was only later on that he told me once that he
had thought I was going to die. I felt a sense of guilt for John's
turmoil too, as if it was my fault.

In May 1994, about a month after the accident, we had another
"faith trip," this time to a beach on a wonderful bay. Tim drove
my car and carried my backpack, which someone had repaired.
All I had to do was be there and everyone made me comfortable. We were talking about what it means to have a calling
from God. I did not have a calling from God that I knew of, but
I wanted one. That weekend I sought the Lord while the others
were doing their activities and God spoke to me. He told me
that the calling He had for my life was from the book of Isaiah
chapter 49. It is an amazing passage. In it God tells Isaiah that he
had been called before his birth and that He had hidden him in
the shadow of His hand, because He was preparing him to be a
light to all the nations and to bring God's salvation to the ends
of the earth. God then speaks of His heart to restore and heal,
assuring Isaiah that although he will suffer the loss of children
and the pain of the bereavement, God will bring recompense.
God promises that those who hope in Him will not be disappointed, and that He will contend with those who contend with
Isaiah and save his children. All of this is to reveal the glory of
the Lord to all mankind. What God had said to Isaiah, I realized
He was now saying to me! I read the chapter over and over and
could not fathom what it really meant. But as you continue to
read my story, bear this in mind and I think you will understand
what God was saying.

Although I did not understand the calling at the time, it was
clearly the highlight of 1994. For the rest of that year I did not
hear God speak. I went through an extremely lonely time still
trying to please the leaders of MTS, but continually feeling like
a failure. David had to leave the choice of what activities I did or
did not do up to me, meaning he could not have complete control over me. My opinion was that he did not like that. I started
to feel the emotion of self-doubt for the first time in my life. I
had come to MTS a confident, independent woman, but bit by
bit my confidence was being eroded. I was desperate for God to

speak to me and help me navigate through the decline. But He was silent. I was alone. The sense that I was wrong, that I was a failure, nagged away at the back of my mind. Compounding it all was my health. I just had pain all the time. Gradually it wore me down too. I remember getting to the point where I said to God, "OK, God, I have had enough now. Could You please take the pain away?" However, it did not go away. The buoyant hope I had known at first was starting to fade.

In July MTS finished. My fellow students were given placements in other countries to get some experience in mission work. Sarah and Josh went to India, Ali went to Uganda and Sam went to Guatemala. Where did I go? Nowhere! David said that I was not ready spiritually to do mission work. Maybe so. My health was not raised as an issue. Overall I was glad I did not go, although I did feel hurt at first. The question was: what do I do now? David suggested that I go back to Sydney and live with some other single young women who had links with their group. So I did. We rented a house together.

By September I decided that the group that had run MTS was not for me. I had given myself wholeheartedly to it. I had tried so hard to fit in and be like them, but I was like a square peg trying to fit into a round hole. They talked about love, but did not show love. They talked about grace, but did not show grace. It is not so much what people say that is important, rather what they do. One night David came to a party at the house where I was living. I was so scared to tell him that I was going to move on but when I told him that I thought the group was not for me, he gave little reply. I am sure he gave a big internal sigh of relief. I felt like I had been the thorn in his side.

I felt a deep sense of betrayal from David and some of the other leaders. They had promised to meet my medical expenses and support me with whatever I needed as a result of the accident. That did not happen. They bought me a prescription on discharge from hospital, got me a new sleeping bag as mine had been lost in the ravine on the night of the accident, and took me to some follow-up appointments or dropped me off at the train so I could go myself. That was the extent of the support I received. There was the possibility that they may have paid some kind of fee for the helicopter, but no one ever confirmed this directly. They never even mentioned to me that they had public liability insurance that could have helped me. I suppose they thought I would be able to work. But they were wrong.

The following year, when I had moved back home, it was very hard for members of not only my close family but also my extended family to see the struggles I was going through. They could see it was a struggle to live on my very limited income and pay my medical expenses. My Great-aunty Lorna became very concerned for my health and welfare and recommended I seek legal advice and consider a public liability claim against the leaders of MTS. I had never done anything like this before and felt daunted at the prospect of a court case. My solicitor at Kenny Spring Solicitors determined their insurance and we decided to start proceedings to file for damages, with the solicitor confident we had a very solid case. I was not 100 per cent sure that I would proceed with it, but it was certainly my legal right given what I had been through, so we started to prepare.

I was still very emotionally damaged from the trauma of MTS, with the consequence that I found it very hard to trust people in authority. Once back in Bathurst I started having Christian counseling, with my primary goal being to forgive David and the other leaders, however long it took. I did not go to a church again until September, when I cautiously started going to the Bathurst Christian Outreach Center, where the pastors were Peter and Alexandra Mann. In fact, on my very first visit to this church – to attend a prophetic conference – God blessed me with a prophetic word from a visiting ministry. The reason that the prophecy spoke so much to me was because it described my journey up until that time so accurately. The Lord said it was as if I had been digging and digging, and that He had formed a well around what I had been doing and that I was going to strike pay dirt soon. He was telling me that I was going to strike gold! This prophetic word had given me a lot of encouragement and the courage to hope again.

Chapter 5

HEALED BY JESUS!

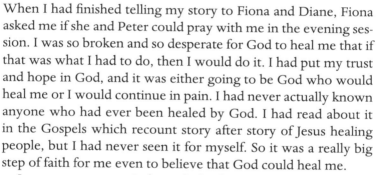

When I had finished telling my story to Fiona and Diane, Fiona asked me if she and Peter could pray with me in the evening session. I was so broken and so desperate for God to heal me that if that was what I had to do, then I would do it. I had put my trust and hope in God, and it was either going to be God who would heal me or I would continue in pain. I had never actually known anyone who had ever been healed by God. I had read about it in the Gospels which recount story after story of Jesus healing people, but I had never seen it for myself. So it was a really big step of faith for me even to believe that God could heal me.

It was a nervous wait through the dinner break. The first part of the evening session was devoted to teaching given by Peter and, when that was finished, he called me up to the front, first inviting me to share with the delegates what had happened to me and what ongoing health consequences I had suffered. As I started to share I was overwhelmed by the love and compassion of those who were there, which I could hear and feel in their response to what I was sharing. I was so moved. There was an audio recording made and even as I listened to it again, as I wrote this chapter, I cried, because I could feel the love in that room at Merroo. I had received very little love and compassion when I fell off that cliff and in the months that followed – it had been a very hard and lonely journey. Through the process of rehabilitation I had come to really dislike doctors, and here I was surrounded by a group of Christian doctors, being loved as I had never been loved before.

I want to share with you as much as I can of what happened next to give you an insight into what God did. I have a recording of the ministry and I am going to go step by step through the process that God took me through to heal my broken heart. This was God's agenda for what He knew I needed to be made whole. Peter and Fiona led the ministry that follows and we had 150 or so witnesses, each one utterly amazed at what they saw.

I was twenty-six years old when this ministry occurred. I was conscious throughout and was able to tell Peter and Fiona what I was feeling or what thoughts were coming to my mind, but as they ministered, it was Lynda aged twenty-three at the bottom of the cliff they addressed and it was she who responded.

Peter speaks to Lynda at twenty-three at the foot of the cliff. I fall on the floor, involuntarily assuming the position I landed in when I fell off the cliff – on my right side, face down. Peter prays that Jesus will lift the trauma out of each part of my body. I start to cry in pain. They continue to pray that Jesus will lift the shock and trauma out. Fiona says, "You are safe, Jesus is here," which is a great comfort to me. Her compassionate female voice touches me in a way I could not have expected. Then my body goes cold as it did at the bottom of the cliff. They cover me with a blanket. Next I start to wail in agony, crying out, "Oh God." I am actually feeling all the physical pain from the fall all over again.

Fiona prays for the blow to my head, that Jesus will bring out the pain and shock to my head, then that He will bring the pain out of the vertebrae, the skin, the muscles and the lacerations.

Next my chest feels compressed and I am feeling pain in my ribs. I cannot breathe and my lungs are feeling squashed, as happened in the hours while I was waiting for the paramedics to reach me. Peter prays that Jesus will expand the lungs and heal them on the inside, and that He will pull the trauma right out of the lungs. I cry in pain again. Then I start to breathe really deeply and feel a release and restoration in my lungs.

Next I feel as if I am drifting into unconsciousness. Fiona prays for the trauma to be lifted out of the unconscious. Speaking directly to the parts that were sent unconscious as I hit my head, Peter commands the demons to release my head and loose my mind and my brain, taking away all the trauma that has been inflicted. Then I ask, "What happened?" Peter tells me that I have fallen down a cliff but that I am now in Jesus' arms and He is healing me. I say, "I don't remember it." After a minute or two I say, "Sing to me," telling them that it would comfort me. They ask what song I would like and I name a song we used to sing at the Missions Training School, "To love only You." No one knows that song, but a lady comes forward and sings "His name is wonderful." I smile and nod my head with joy. Next I ask to have someone read Psalm 23, as they did when I was at the bottom of the cliff. Fiona reads it to me and it brings a great sense of comfort also. She then starts praying for God to take away the sense of abandonment that I felt at the time of the fall and to show me that I am covered with love, that I am safe and that everything is going to be all right. I then feel at peace.

I am aware next that I cannot feel my back hurting. Then my leg starts twitching involuntarily. The pain comes back in my lower back, on the right side. Fiona then takes authority over any demonic power in the areas where there is pain. Any spirits of infirmity or sickness are commanded to come right out in Jesus' name, loosing the legs, the spine, the nerves. She then prays for the side of the body that took the impact of the fall, asking Jesus to heal that area as well as the head, which also took the impact. She commands any demonic power to come right off that place. I start feeling a lot of pain. Fiona continues praying for the spirit of pain, injury and accident to come out of me in Jesus' name. Peter then takes authority over the spirit of curse, commanding it to come out through my breath in Jesus' name. Peter also commands spirits of shock and trauma to come right out. Starting from the bottom of my spine and moving upwards, I feel a strong crushing sensation as the demons first come to the surface and then leave my body. Peter commands the spirits of infirmity to leave. Next I make a declaration, "I want to live."

The pain starts getting stronger. Peter anoints me with oil in the name of the Father, the Son and the Holy Spirit. I continue to feel pain. Then I start breathing deeply and with each breath I am being delivered of demonic power. I feel a release. I then feel light in the head. Fiona prays that the spirit and soul that were broken apart at the time of the accident will be brought together again. The feeling of unconsciousness comes over me again. Fiona reassures me that I am safe and that Jesus is still there with me, ministering His healing to me. She speaks His healing into my head, into my soul and into my spirit. My head starts hurting again. I say that this is the headache that I get regularly. Fiona prays for Jesus to release all the demonic power that came with the blow to the head. My head is very hot. Peter prays that Jesus will lift off all the demonic trauma that is attached to the head. He then prays that where my mind has been shattered and broken, Jesus will bring it back together again.

I am then aware of twitching all down my left leg and pain all around the right side of my head. Fiona takes authority over all demonic power, commanding anything demonic that is attached to the part of the brain that controls the left side of the body to come out. My head is still red hot. I am feeling "dopey." The deliverance continues gently as I breathe out. Then my head goes cool very suddenly. The headache is also gone. I can feel the anointing of the Holy Spirit.

I feel tingling going up and down my back. Fiona again takes authority over any demonic power, forbidding it to torment me, and asks for Jesus' healing power to come upon me and set me free. The pain comes back again, starting at my back, then reaching down my leg, right down to my foot. Fiona prays for Jesus to take the trauma away. I feel very warm between my shoulder blades. As she continues to pray, I have further deliverance, breathing deeply and releasing the demons that I never knew I had.

Bit by bit Jesus was releasing me from everything that held me bound.

Once I had been delivered, I started undergoing healing. On the recording I can hear all the amazed sounds of those who were there watching what God was doing to me. Those watching say I was having traction by angels as I was stretched into some amazing positions that I could not have achieved on my own. I felt as if I was receiving supernatural massage – I could feel my body being pulled and stretched (although I didn't see it as my eyes remained closed throughout the ministry). At one point, as I lay on the floor on my stomach, my arms were pulled back behind me and my legs were pulled upwards, so that I grasped my ankles with my hands – it was incredible! My body felt wonderful for the first time in a very long while. At this stage in the ministry I saw Jesus' face before me in a vision. He was smiling at me, and I started to laugh.

> *I feel a lot of pain in the lower torso. Fiona prays for peace and comfort to this part of my body that took the impact of the fall. She drives out every power of the enemy that came in through this injury. Suddenly my head feels very tight as if a band has been tightened around it. Peter blesses some water and puts it around my head in a ring. He then breaks all demonic hold upon my head in Jesus' name and asks Jesus to release healing into my head. Fiona then breaks the curse of death.*
>
> *Peter then receives a specific word of knowledge for me. He says, "In the name of Jesus I want to break the assignment that Satan had to destroy your calling under God through this accident and I break that curse upon you now." He then speaks a restoration of my calling into my spirit and prays that I will be a hundred times more powerful for Jesus because of what I have seen Him do in my life. The tight band around my head then goes.*
>
> *I have pain in my right ear. This was the side of my head that took the impact of the fall. Fiona prays that Jesus will remove any residual impact on my ear, the sound of falling, the noise of hitting the ground. Peter takes authority over any demonic power affecting my ear and my forehead and asks Jesus to bring healing.*
>
> *Then I have a sense that I am going to be crushed from above. Fiona prays against this fear. I know exactly where this fear springs*

*from: I feel as if the leaders at the Missions Training School want
to crush me (I am thinking specifically of David). The hike itself
was all about dying to yourself and supposedly having to trust
Jesus. I do not know how to explain the context of the accident
to Peter and Fiona, so Fiona moves on to the atmosphere and the
people around me at the bottom of the cliff, thinking that was
the crushing sensation. All the people from the Missions Training
School thought that I was going to die. She prays I will be released
from the influence of that atmosphere of fear and death from those
with me. Peter then prays that Jesus will break the ties between
me and the group I was with and asks Jesus to deliver me from
all the powers of darkness that came upon me and especially that
gained access to me through the accident and through the people
that came around me at that time. He commands the spiritual
oppression to be lifted off me in Jesus' name.*

*Then the issue of forgiveness of the leader of the Training
School (and the leader of the hike) comes into focus. Peter says to
me, "Can you forgive David, Lynda?"*

I knew in those few moments that I had to forgive, even though
I had been hurt so much. All the counseling I had received came
down to this. I also knew that when I forgave I had to let it go,
no more talking about it or complaining about it. It was finished.
I was also aware that if I did not forgive at that moment when
Jesus gave me the opportunity, the healing would be stalled right
there. So that night I let it go and I forgave David.

*In Jesus' name Peter cuts me off from that leader and his influ-
ence, and from the control of his organization, and severs the
emotional soul-tie. This is a greatly liberating part of the ministry for me. The sense of crushing is gone.*

*The next thing I feel is nausea. Fiona prays that Jesus will
bring out the trauma and the feelings of being sick from the shock
and the impact of the accident. She prays for my stomach and
I start having more deep deliverance. Then Fiona asks Jesus to
heal my stomach, as well as anything that brought sickness to my
emotions. I can feel something coming up my throat. I breathe out
deeply a number of times. Then I can feel something going down*

my throat. I say, "It feels like healing going down my esophagus." One of the doctors jokes in the background that "It's a spiritual endoscopy!" Fiona prays that Jesus will heal all the stomach ulcers and the lining of the stomach where there has been fear and trauma. I say, "I can feel it right from my throat down to my stomach." Fiona prays that Jesus will re-create my stomach the way He intended it to be, giving me back life and health and strength in Jesus' name. The Holy Spirit continues moving in my stomach.

Fiona pauses in the ministry to give grateful thanks to the Lord for what He is doing and to tell Jesus that we love Him, we trust Him and we worship Him, giving Him all the glory.

I start feeling pain in my head again. Peter prays that Jesus will restore the muscle control functions originating in the brain, and restore all damage that was done to the whole of the motor system and all of the nervous reactions. He prays that Jesus will bring His restoration so that all communication may be totally restored to the brain and so that there will be no loss of function in any part of the body. At this point the pain gets stronger. Peter then takes authority over any demonic power affecting the control of the nerves in the head which has been forced to manifest. He tells it to go, breaking its hold in Jesus' name. I then start coughing vigorously and have further deliverance. Peter drives out all the demonic powers behind the accident, commanding them to go in Jesus' name, making specific reference to the spirits of death. I continue breathing out very deeply. He breaks the hold of spirits affecting the whole of the nervous system, including spirits of paralysis. Fiona speaks Jesus' life into my lungs. Peter rebukes any future rheumatism or arthritis. My breathing settles, but my head is still a bit painful. Peter lays his hand directly on the part of my head where I am experiencing pain, asking the Lord to pour His anointing through his hand to drive out any demonic power that remains. He rebukes all the curses of death, destruction, paralysis and all future diseases through which the demonic powers might seek to exercise control over me. Expanding on that, he prays that the Lord will flush right out of every part of my body all the demonic curses of sickness and infirmity which are residing there waiting to attack me in later years. He asks Jesus *to take them right away, off every bodily organ, off every bodily system. He tells the demons to manifest and go in Jesus' name. I say "No," repeating it five times, getting louder each time – the demon is speaking through me. Peter places the demon under the authority of the Lord Jesus Christ of Nazareth.*

Fiona then starts to cut me off from any generational curse of infirmity or sickness that may have been strengthened through the accident, and she tells it to come right out in Jesus' name. She cuts me off from my generational line on my mother's side and my father's side in Jesus' name. She then declares that I have an inheritance in Christ Jesus and tells the demon to come right out, breaking the generational curse in the mighty name of the Lord Jesus. She commands the demon to leave both sides of the family line. Then as I breathe out deeply again the demon goes. Peter also adds that all the fears of future sickness have got to go out with it. Peter discerns that this has been the deepest deliverance of them all. Although they started ministering into the accident, God has moved into much deeper generational issues that needed to be dealt with. This deliverance goes on for some minutes. Fiona starts speaking the life of Jesus to me and asks the Lord to fill up with His Holy Spirit those places vacated by the demonic power.

Next I have pain right in the front of my head. Fiona asks the Lord to reveal to us what it is that is causing the pain. I feel a witness within me that it is something coming from my generational line. Peter asks me if I will forgive all my ancestors for the sins they committed that have affected me. I say, "I do." Peter then separates between my mother's line and my father's line and in the name of Jesus Christ of Nazareth takes authority over all the demonic power that has come down my generational line on my mother's side of the family, commanding it to come out now. He binds all the demonic power coming down my father's side of the family and tells it too to come out in the name of Jesus Christ of Nazareth. Instantly my head is being forced to the ground and Peter can barely hold it up. He discerns that this is worship of false gods from my mother's family line. He breaks the power of worship of false gods on the generational line, and tells the demon to come out because it cannot have me. He forbids the demon to bow its head onto the ground to serve false gods, declaring that "Lynda serves the Lord Jesus Christ." I have the sense that the demon has got something to do with sexual sin on the generational line. Peter asks, "Lynda, do you want Jesus to be Lord of your sexuality?" I say "yes." As he prays for me, a picture comes into my mind of a person I knew, who many years before had been involved in sexual sin. It was not a situation of abuse, but out of respect for that person's privacy I won't be more specific here. Peter prays into that situation and Jesus unlocks the demonic hold of sexual curse that had been affecting me both from my generational line and from this situation. I again undergo deep deliverance. The headache goes. Fiona asks the Lord to fill that place with the Holy Spirit, declaring that my body is a temple of the Holy Spirit. She then prays for rightful and godly relationships for me.

Peter continues praying about my generational lines. He asks me if I forgive everyone on my father's side of the family, including my father. I do. In the name of Jesus Christ of Nazareth he then breaks the spirit, soul and body tie between me and my father and all the ungodly ties that exist in my generational line, asking the Lord to take away from me every ungodly spirit that has been down the generational line which has affected me through my father's side of the family. I start to feel really angry with my dad.

I had a lot of emotional pain and anger inside of me that I did not realize was there. I loved my dad very much, as any daughter would, and I knew he loved me and would do anything for me. I became aware that, at a very deep level, I was disappointed that he had not been able to provide me with the emotional and spiritual support that I so desperately needed in my formative years. This changed as the years went on. But at this moment in the ministry I was hurting and I needed to forgive my dad. I knew he had never meant to hurt me. Only Jesus held the key to unlock the pain and release us both. As I forgave, the key started to turn.

Fiona then prays that God will deliver me from any spirits that had come down to me through my father's line. I continue to feel

emotional pain. Peter prays that Father God will pour His heal-
ing into every hurt that there had been from my human father.
He then prays for healing from every hurt that has come down
the generational line from the way people on my father's side of
the family have treated one another through the generations, for
all the cruelty, the wrongful punishment and the wrong attitudes.
From a few stories I had heard from past generations this was
a very accurate word of knowledge from the Holy Spirit. Peter
breaks their hold in Jesus' name.

I get another strong pain, right in the temple. As Peter prays I
know in my spirit that there is a spirit of fatherlessness on Dad's
side of the family. They had physical fathers, but they were men
who had difficulty in teaching their sons to be men. My dad was like
that. But I never knew there was a demonic spirit behind it, intent
on robbing our family of strong godly men. Peter breaks the power of
all the spirits of fatherlessness in Jesus' name and asks Father God to
come and be the rightful father. He prays about all the pain, loneli-
ness and isolation of a child growing up without a father and asks
the Lord to release me of it. I again start having deliverance, cough-
ing for a short time. Immediately the pain is gone!

Peter asks the Lord if there is anything else He wants to do
before we finish praying. I can feel Jesus' hand on my back and it
is very hot where He is touching me. Then I feel pain on my left
hip. A few minutes go by. Peter asks what is happening. I can feel
warmth all over my lower back and it is moving down my left
side. Fiona gives thanks to the Lord for what He is doing. The
warmth continues for some minutes as the Holy Spirit continues
to bring healing. Next I feel a stretching in my lower back. I have
no pain anywhere in my body!

Peter asks my permission for the next stage, which I give. He
reminds everyone that I am still Lynda at twenty-three years of
age and it is only by the power of the Lord Jesus that I can be
grown up to become one with the 26-year-old Lynda. He gives
thanks to the Lord Jesus for what He has done for Lynda at
twenty-three, that Jesus was there when I had the accident and
that He remembered everything that needed to be dealt with.
Peter asks Jesus to take 23-year-old Lynda by the hand and grow

me safely through those years to the age of twenty-six, which big
Lynda is now. He asks Jesus supernaturally to draw those two
parts together, so that instead of there being two parts of Lynda
there will only be one. He asks that as Jesus draws those two parts
together, He would seal me with His Holy Spirit. Peter declares
into the heavenly realm that what Jesus has joined together, no
man, demon, evil spirit or power of darkness may put asunder,
and that my complete healing to my spirit, soul and body will be
living testimony to the power of the Lord Jesus Christ.

I stood up and opened my eyes and saw everyone in the room
sitting in a big semi-circle around me, beaming at me with the biggest smiles. It was awesome. I was vaguely aware of what had happened, but it felt as if it was "back there," three years ago. The one
thing that I remember above all when I stood up from the floor
was that the "broken" feeling that had wrecked my life for the past
three years was gone! I had a tangible sense that all the broken
pieces inside of me had been put back together, like when a jigsaw
is completed. It was so amazing! Jesus had healed me in my body,
but also in my soul and spirit. All three were connected.

One of my other clear memories of when I got up from the
floor was seeing my room-mate Diane with a great big smile on
her face. She had told me that she would have to leave during the
evening session and so when I saw that she was still there, I
was absolutely thrilled that she had seen Jesus heal me. Not only
that but God in His amazing timing had brought her husband
Paul to the meeting that night and he had witnessed the amazing
ministry also. I hurried over and gave her a big hug, which was a
pivotal moment in her life, as she explains in the next chapter.

To complete this incredible night we all burst into song, singing the old hymn "Praise my soul, the King of Heaven." We gave
God all the thanks, praise and glory for what He had done. I
could not wait to get to a phone, even at 11 pm, to ring my parents and tell them I had been healed. I only wished they could
have been there to share it with me. On 18 September 1996 Jesus
totally changed my life and many of the lives of those who were
there. Praise God!

Chapter 6

AND THEY WERE ALL AMAZED!

In the Gospels we see time and time again that the people were amazed when they saw Jesus healing the sick or casting out demons. In Luke 9:43 we read, for example, "And they were all amazed at the greatness of God." Peter had pointed these verses out to us as he had been teaching about Jesus' healing ministry. After everyone had seen what had happened to me, they started calling out, "The people were all amazed!" It became like the catch cry of the conference.

My healing made such an impact on the lives of the people who were there that night that I have asked some of them to write down what they saw and heard. They not only substantiate my account but they also demonstrate the ripple-effect it had in many people's lives.

Testimony of Dr Gregory Foote

M.B., B.S., F.R.A.C.G.P.

Attending the first Ellel Conference at Merroo, sponsored by Health Care In Christ, was a very exciting time for my wife and me. We had teaching from Peter Horrobin at Ellel Grange in 1990 and were very impressed.

Before the ministry, I noticed that Lynda looked really ill. She had dark shadows under her eyes, marked weight loss, her face was pale, and her hair lacked luster. I was surprised when Fiona Horrobin said to me, "I believe God is going to perform a miracle tonight." Being medical, I thought, "I am going to get at the front, to get a good view of what is happening; I want to be sure that this is real."

When the ministry started, Lynda fell on the floor, lying face down (prone position), which is most likely the position she was in when she spent the night in the bush, after the fall. As the ministry continued, I saw Lynda's spine start to move; head and shoulders, knees and feet bent upward, *beyond* the normal limit. It looked like her spine was being stretched by a heavenly chiropractor. There was much deliverance, particularly from the effect of negative words spoken by people on the training team and rescue team.

Lynda forgave the training school leadership. There was breaking of ungodly soul-ties with the leader who had put pressure on Lynda to go on the hike at night. At one stage the ministry stopped, and Peter Horrobin was unsure of the hindrance. Lynda spoke up that there was someone she had to forgive and talked about the situation briefly.

When she forgave, the ministry continued gently, with Peter and Fiona praying quietly, encouraging Lynda. The 150 delegates at the conference were all praying at the same time. There were many doctors and other medical and pastoral people present.

The ministry went on for approximately two hours, starting at 9.00 pm. I am a morning person, and normally am going to bed at this time, but I was *wide awake*! Lynda stood up and said that she did not have any pain in her back, a miracle in itself. My faith was strong before this conference, but it rose to a whole new level after seeing Lynda's healing. I said to her, "Touch your toes!", which she did rapidly, and without effort. I knew God had healed her.

The next morning Lynda told us how she had slowly walked up the hill to the Prayer House at Merroo, to thank God for her healing. The day before she would have walked a couple of steps, gritted her teeth with pain before taking more steps. However, this time she slowly walked without pain.

Next day Peter prayed for Lynda to be released from any adverse effects from the anesthetics and the medications which she had taken for pain relief.

One year later we saw Lynda at the Waterloo conference, where she gave her testimony. I was amazed to see this beautiful young lady, tall, straight, healthy color in her cheeks, and shiny fair hair in a ponytail. She looked five years younger!

Testimony of Roslyn Curry, Physiotherapist

I was one of 150 people who were perched in quite precarious positions watching in awe and silence as the Lord Jesus Christ healed Lynda. I had actually slid under a chair that someone else was standing on. None of us moved from our vantage point for the whole two hours that the Lord ministered to her, systematically healing one part of her body after another. As a physiotherapist, I was amazed at the Lord realigning her spine with traction without using any apparatus. He also manipulated her joints especially her shoulders, lifting her arms in an arc above her head.

It was amazing to see the Lord healing her whole being and to see that healing and deliverance, occurring on a spiritual plane, was impacting her physical body. Even more amazing was the way that the Lord went back to the root of Lynda's problems to the very accident itself, so that she experienced the same physical, emotional and spiritual things that she had experienced at that time and He then systematically healed each injury and the associated trauma. Whenever there was a blockage to the healing process, the Lord gave Peter and Fiona discernment to deal with generational iniquities on her family line and other issues such as a need for forgiveness of the leaders responsible for the hike in the dark. The Lord was so gracious as He challenged all of us watching to a new appreciation of His love, mercy and grace while very carefully demolishing our medical mindsets.

This was our first experience of an Ellel seminar and it was a baptism of fire that has been indelibly burned into our memory. We were not sure of what to expect when we invited Peter and Fiona Horrobin to come and speak to us on evangelism, healing and deliverance. We knew that these three biblical principles were significant for health care as they are the themes of Luke 10, the foundational chapter for Health Care In Christ. However, we were unaware that the Lord wanted to impart to us a new understanding of His Kingdom in health care that would have a far-reaching effect on each of our lives and on our future direction as a ministry. We now see it as a turning point for us and HCIC and the beginnings of an exciting journey with Peter, Fiona, Jill Southern and Ellel.

When I first met Lynda, I was impressed by her gentle spirit, humility and love for the Lord, but when I saw her walk up the hill to the prayer tower at Merroo the day after her healing, I saw a new Lynda walking freely and filled with joy. The Lord imparted that joy to each of us and inspired us to seek Him, to see health care transformed by His Holy Spirit just as we had seen Lynda's life transformed.

Testimony of Dr Ken Curry

M.B., B.S. Hons., D.T.M.H., M.Med.Ed., F.A.Ch.A.M.

I approached the Evangelism, Healing and Deliverance conference with Ellel Ministries in 1996 with some fear and trepidation. Dr John Ouw, then the Health Care In Christ leader in Victoria and a psychiatrist, had said to me that to understand mental illness we must understand deliverance. That is why he invited Peter Horrobin to come and teach and minister in Australia. I agreed but when it came time to go, as a doctor, to the conference I had lots of fears and doubts that arose within me.

The night that Lynda was healed was a night of a major paradigm shift for me and I think for many others, especially the many health workers who stood around watching God at work. I remember well the nature of the teaching by Peter Horrobin complete with the illustration of the bus running over the person and the explanation that trauma causes not only physical injury but also trauma to the soul and spirit. Peter and Fiona then used Lynda's trauma to illustrate their teaching in most remarkable ways. They prayed through so many things from the initial experience of the accident and lying overnight at the bottom of the cliff with healing and deliverance one after the other. Physical symptoms were prayed through with amazing manifestations like "traction" and stretching of her spine, muscles, joints and bones being restored to wholeness. At one stage I remember Lynda saying she felt like something was going down into her stomach, like an endoscopy tube and then a healing in her stomach from an ulcer she had been suffering. There was also prayer about operations and procedures. There was forgiveness for those who had hurt her. Depression was also lifting. All this prayer and ministry followed the pattern of deliverance and healing, deliverance and healing. Next day I heard that Lynda had been able to walk up the hill to the Prayer House, which was a level of exercise that she had not been able to accomplish since the accident. I had known Lynda through HCIC before the accident. It was such a joy to see her being restored to the vivacious young woman that she had been before the accident.

One of the memories is of so many health workers – doctors, nurses, physiotherapists and so on – standing around with eyes agog as to what was going on. One thought I had was that this was a new dimension of which previously I had had very little understanding. I thought of so many of the patients that I saw and other health workers saw on a daily basis. I realized that there is so much going on in the spiritual realm that as health practitioners we have no training or understanding about. There is so much more to learn and so much more to experience that God has for His people. All glory to God for His wonderful healing and for the keys that He has revealed to His faithful servants. Our heart is that more and more Christian health workers will grow in understanding and ministry of the fullness of God's freedom and healing.

Testimony of Dr Catherine Hayes

B. Med. [Hons.], Newcs., D.R.C.O.G.[U.K.],

Dip. Psych.Onc.[Melb.]

As I reflect on witnessing the beautiful healing miracle that Lynda experienced, I realize that the events of that weekend have deeply impacted the way I practice medicine and my personal journey with God.

In my work in medicine I have met many people like Lynda who have survived major trauma, but have failed to recover their previous level of health and vitality. Learning that trauma is experienced at all levels of our body, soul and spirit was a transformational concept for me.

When Peter and Fiona began to pray for Lynda they prayed for her back at the time of the accident. It was as if we time-traveled with the Holy Spirit and Lynda began to re-experience the trauma of her accident. As a medic it was interesting to me that Lynda behaved from this point exactly as you would expect someone with her injuries to do. Her posture and the way she drifted in and out of consciousness were totally consistent with the injuries she received. I was amazed that through prayer we could invite Jesus to minister to some previous time in our history.

As Lynda drifted in and out of consciousness she asked Fi to sing to her. This spoke to me about the power of music to connect with our Spirit. It also showed me how aware and sensitive our Spirit is even when we are unconscious. Now, whenever I am around patients with altered levels of consciousness I am aware of my ability to minister to their spirit. In these situations I will also speak to the patient's family and let them know that the patient is very aware of the things they say and do at the bedside.

I remember watching as Lynda's body was moved into different stretches and postures by unseen hands. The atmosphere in the room at that time was one of awe; we were all aware that we were standing on holy ground.

I was deeply challenged in the later session when I realized that medication could in some circumstances create dependence and bondage. I prescribe medication routinely as part of my work. I had to prayerfully consider this. Now I commit my day to God and where appropriate I encourage patients to pray over new medication.

The final major lesson for me was the harm we can do as practitioners when we fail to recognize that the physical things that we are asked to treat, are just part of a bigger picture. Everyone we see is a whole being whose illness may reflect the need for healing at all levels of their being, body, soul and spirit.

These are just some ways that the ripples spread out from Lynda's deep healing miracle into my own life.

Testimony of Paul Watson

The Ellel Ministries' four-day course held at Merroo Conference Center in September 1996 changed my life forever. My wife Diane really felt that she was to attend this and as I waved good-bye to her in the car park I sensed that there was a big change coming. On the evening of the third day I returned to Merroo to have dinner with Diane at the course, to sit in on the evening session, and to take Diane home afterwards.

Being an Anglican minister trained in the Sydney Diocese, I was quite unsure about what this ministry organization was teaching, so I was keen to hear for myself.

That night Peter Horrobin was teaching on healing that can come for victims of accidents and other traumas in their life. It certainly was interesting, if not very unusual to my theological training and perspective. There were about 150 people present, and the vast majority came from the medical professions. Peter and Fiona Horrobin invited Lynda to come forward and began to speak with her, inviting her to share her story with us. They then began to pray and minister to her. It was a whole new experience for me, and I watched in amazement – from my vantage point up on a desk – as God was working His miraculous healing in Lynda's body, soul and spirit. I had never seen anything like this before. We weren't used to looking for the miraculous in my church experiences!

After the ministry was over, and Lynda had hugged Diane and said goodbye, I drove Diane and another person home to Sydney. We had a very lively conversation on the way. What I had heard, seen and experienced needed to be processed through my biblical viewpoint. I could see that Diane was very excited that she had found a ministry that really touched her heart. And Lynda was healed!

I know that God orchestrated my being present that night, as I probably would not have believed what had happened if I had not been there to see it for myself. What an amazing night! Praise God!

Testimony of Diane Watson

I had come to this HCIC event not knowing what to expect; all I knew was that God very strongly prompted me to be there. At the time I was an Anglican vicar's wife. I shared a room with five other ladies, one of whom was Lynda. I had come to the conference not knowing anyone, but Lynda and I just clicked. I remember just the second day after meeting Lynda, she asked for a hug. I guess I was like a mum figure to her and I felt very at ease with her. Our friendship grew over those three days, but most significant was being there to experience Lynda's healing.

I was leaving on the Wednesday night as I had four children at home and I felt I could not stay any longer. But that was the night of Lynda's ministry and she had asked if I would be there for her as she was feeling very vulnerable about going on stage for the upfront ministry. I said I would stay for it. My husband Paul, who came to pick me up, was also there to witness what happened.

Through the teaching and ministry of Ellel Ministries at this conference, I felt for the first time in my twenty years of being a Christian that I was hearing truth about healing and spiritual issues that resonated with my spirit.

As Peter and Fiona prayed into the accident Lynda fell into the position into which she had fallen when she was at the bottom of the cliff – that was amazing, but what really stood out for me was watching as Lynda was being physically healed by "angels." Her back and legs looked like they were being manipulated by invisible hands and her muscles rippled as her back, arms and legs were being aligned into place. It is the most incredible thing I have ever seen.

There were lots of aspects to Lynda's healing, forgiveness, deliverance and physical healing that were amazing. Even more amazing, however, was when, after two hours, Lynda rose from the ministry, her beautiful blue eyes sparkling, and came and gave me a hug as she knew I was leaving. Peter had asked that everyone would give Lynda space and not all come and hug her, as she was exhausted after the ministry, but she came and hugged me. As she did, I felt God say to me, "I have chosen you for this ministry." It was quite overwhelming. I had no clue as to what that would involve.

Testimony of Peter Horrobin

When my wife and I first talked to Lynda about the possibility of praying for her healing, she was less than enthusiastic! She had been prayed for many times before and hadn't been healed. She didn't want to experience any further disappointment, and the prospect of yet again not being healed was more than she wanted to bear.

But as Fiona talked with her about the understandings God had given us of inner brokenness that can accompany the consequences of a physical accident, God gave her hope and the faith to believe once again for her healing. She came to realize that when Isaiah had said that the Sovereign Lord would heal the broken-hearted (Isaiah 61:1), she was included in the promise.

Lynda took a very courageous step when she climbed on the small platform that night, and in front of many doctors and other medical practitioners put her trust in God afresh. We had no idea what God was going to do, but we did know that if all those medics were going to be impacted by the love and power of God to heal, they needed to see something real happening!

Through the work of Ellel Ministries, we had seen God move in great power in many people's lives, bringing profound healing to spirit, soul and body. But we'd also had to walk through many years of skepticism, opposition and rejection from people inside and outside the Church who did not understand that what Jesus did on earth through healing and deliverance, He was still doing today.

We had never prayed for healing before in a meeting that was almost exclusively made up of medical practitioners! All we could do was to trust the God who had been so faithful in the past, to bring His healing love and power into Lynda's life. It was an extraordinary and unforgettable privilege to participate that night with God, in His healing of Lynda's broken life. Seeing this young woman, whose only future at that time was the prospect of a lifetime of disability, be restored to wholeness once again, was one of those experiences which will remain in the memory as a permanent reminder of God's faithfulness – and a constant encouragement to keep on praying for those in need.

A very significant element in Lynda's healing was her own personal love for and absolute trust in God – along with the prayers of everyone in the room as they watched what God was doing. It was a life-transforming experience for every one of us who were present, especially for many of the medics, whose whole perspective of medicine and healing took a huge step forward in understanding. No amount of teaching or persuasion could have done for those doctors what God did in those two dramatic hours, as they watched Him at work. But having seen and testified to what He did, none of us could ever be the same again!

Testimony of Fiona Horrobin

In our work, we have seen many people come into profound physical and emotional healing following accidents and traumas of various kinds. One of the vital keys is forgiveness of ourselves, of others and of God. Blaming God is a common thread in some people's thinking and their thoughts go along the lines of, "Why did God allow this to happen?" – rarely giving thought to the free will of mankind and that all of us often suffer the consequences of our own sin or that of others.

Then there is the matter of genuine mistakes which have no bad motive at the root. These things can be tough to come to terms with and releasing the emotional trauma and pain to God brings a healing to the inner being, which no amount of physical medicine can do for you. When the inside person receives healing and freedom from spiritual bondage, we have found that the Holy Spirit of God will often heal physically as well.

I think many people miss out on the healing that God wants to bring because they do not want to be real and face the pain which lies at the root of their ongoing problem, whether it is physical pain, spiritual pain or mental/emotional pain. By the time we began to pray for her, Lynda was willing without any reserve to walk with God through the accident and the trauma she had suffered. As the Holy Spirit brought to the surface of her conscious mind the memory of what had happened, Lynda re-lived painful aspects of it in her journey to full healing. There is no doubt that her trust in God for the courage to do so was vital.

We give Him all the glory for Lynda's healing. What a great God who knows each of us personally and fully! He is the best surgeon and doctor of the soul. He is the Creator and knows best how we are made. Psalm 139 tells us that we are fearfully and wonderfully made. Who better to go to when things are in disorder but to the Maker Himself. Lynda is a living testimony to His grace, love and power to heal.

Chapter 7

THE NEXT DAY

———————— ≈ ————————

The next morning I woke up at 6.10 am. Waking so early was highly unusual for me – I usually slept as late as I could to conserve my energy. Although I had only had about six hours' sleep, I felt wide awake, my mind reliving the events of the previous evening. I thought I would get up and go for a walk. It was a beautiful, mild spring morning, with clear blue skies and the sun rising over the hills. It was the first sunrise I had seen in a very long time! The Conference Center had a Prayer House on a small hill close by and I thought I would try to make it there. That was the first step I took in walking out my healing. It was a step of faith, doing something I would never have attempted previously.

I walked right to the top of the hill without even one twitch of back pain! I stopped only once to give my lungs a break as I was a bit out of condition, but my back felt great. The last time I had walked with such freedom I had been on that nightmare hike in pitch blackness. My heart was ready to explode with joy. A healing I had hardly dared to hope for had happened. There was an ease in my body I had not experienced for such a long time. I had never felt so released and so free in all my life. I wanted to hop, skip and jump for joy, but for now I contented myself with walking at a nice steady pace. My heart danced as

I looked across the magnificent green hills with the morning sun rising on them. I felt alive again for the first time since the accident, really alive.

When I got to the Prayer House I spent time with Jesus. So intimate was the love I felt in His presence that morning that I felt like a bride entering the bridal chamber to be with her lover. To this day I can still remember it. I asked Jesus if there was anything He wanted to say to me. In response, whether it was a vision I do not know, I saw Jesus standing before me and He was smiling at me as He had during the ministry the night before. I sat there basking in Jesus' beautiful presence and love.

At breakfast everyone wanted to know how I was feeling. There was an excited buzz around the place and again I felt very touched by the love and warmth of everyone there. Everybody now felt like my new best friends – there was a shared intimacy between us which had grown as they had journeyed with me through my ministry and poured out their hearts in love and compassion towards me, in empathy for the suffering I had endured. I knew that I was going to be given an opportunity in the morning session to tell people how I was feeling and my response to what had happened to me. Everyone could not wait to hear how I was feeling.

Although I did not voice it publically, there was one question at the back of my mind. I couldn't help wondering why during the ministry I had reacted emotionally and physically in the way that I had – the feelings of hot and cold, the pains in various parts of my body, the different emotions, the stretching of my body. Was it me making it up? Well, amazingly, God had an answer for me that I would not have expected. One of my other room-mates at the conference was a young woman named Jasmine, with beautiful long blonde hair and a lovely smile. She was a social worker. Before the meeting that morning Jasmine took me to one side, saying that there was something she just had to tell me about the night before. She told me that throughout the whole ministry she had felt everything in her body and soul that I was feeling – before I felt it! She had been sitting next to a doctor named Bruce and had been giving him a running commentary in advance of all that was happening in the ministry! Wow! God has no half measures. God set up His own confirmation that everything that happened in the ministry on that night was of Him.

Resuming the teaching that morning Peter talked about how drugs, especially those that affect the central nervous system, can have demonic power behind them. This was a particularly challenging concept for many of the doctors and health professionals, whose livelihood revolves around the use of drugs. Sensing that it was an area that had not been covered the previous evening, Peter decided to pray with me again. Most unexpectedly we went into a second session of ministry. I had not had any general anesthesia as a result of the accident, but I had been given a myriad of very strong intravenous drugs, including pain relief and antibiotics. Later, when I was suffering with the stomach ulcers, I was given anesthetics for the gastroscopy procedure. All of these drugs had had a bearing on me that I had not realized.

Peter commands any spirits attached to any of the drugs that I had been given to come to the surface, to come right out of my mind and all the bodily organs affected by the drugs. He breaks the hold of any demonic power upon the drugs from the manufacturers, from the prescribers, from everyone associated with the giving of those drugs, and he asks Jesus to lift those things off me now. My hand goes numb, from my thumb right up to my wrist. Peter comes against any demonic power that has affected me as a result of drugs that have been administered at my left wrist. (This is where an intravenous drip was inserted due to my broken right elbow.) Fiona prays against the effect that these drugs may have had on the spirit and the soul and asks Jesus to set me free. They pray for Jesus to cleanse my bloodstream. My thumb continues to be numb. Peter prays that the demonic power of the anesthetic will come right out of me in Jesus' name. As Peter says this, I fall to the ground. Fiona prays into the trauma of the treatment I suffered at the hospital and prays for the Lord to lift off from my spirit and soul any shock or trauma through that time, making specific mention of shock from injections or catheters inserted in my arm. In Jesus' name she comes against any spirit of death that came on me or any spirit of mind control. I feel as if I am being squashed. Peter prays against any words that were spoken over me while I was unconscious. Fiona breaks any soul-tie that was established with anyone with any wrong intention of heart.

Peter then takes authority in the name of Jesus over the spirit of anesthesia and tells the spirit that came in through anesthesia to come right out of my consciousness now. It is to come out of my bloodstream and lift off my consciousness. I then lapse into semi-consciousness. Peter explains that as demons attached to anesthetics come to the surface the person usually gets anesthetized again.

Next I have a pulsating pain in my bowel. Fiona prays for the Lord's healing of my digestive system. She prays for God to bring His alignment to my body where it has been distressed. I feel like my bowel is "angry." One of the delegates who is an anesthetist comes forward and explains that the anesthetic can sometimes diffuse into the bowel and cause distress in the bowel area. Fiona prays for peace in the name of Jesus and comfort to the bowel. She also prays into any inner anger in my emotions about what happened or what is happening to me, asking Jesus to release it. The pain continues. Peter specifically mentions the names of some of the drugs I had been given. In Jesus' name he looses any demonic power attached to the nitrous oxide I received in the anesthesia. As soon as Peter says "nitrous oxide" my head droops over.

At that point the recording of the ministry ends. Peter decided to release the conference for their break while Fiona continued ministering to me, with the help of the anesthetist I mentioned, Dr Chris Hayes. I have included what happened up till now to help you understand the powerful effect drugs can have on the spirit, soul and body. While they are clearly of great benefit, they can be used by Satan to gain a stronghold over us. I remember hearing Dr Chris going through all the drugs he could think of that may have been administered to me and praying for the Lord to release me of any ungodly influence from them. I underwent further deliverance and then healing as Jesus set me free from the effect of many different drugs.

I have asked Dr Chris to share how the ministry I received over both days impacted him most as a doctor and an anesthetist, in particular the ministry into drugs and anesthetics.

Testimony of Dr Chris Hayes

F.A.N.Z.C.A. F.F.P.M.A.N.Z.C.A.

In being invited by Lynda to provide a medical perspective on her story I find myself readily drifting back to 1996 and that conference room at Merroo where a remarkable healing took place. The events of that time challenged my understanding of trauma and recovery and have continued to impact the way that I practice medicine to this day.

In 1996 I was undertaking a year of training in pain medicine at Royal North Shore Hospital in Sydney. I had completed my training as an anesthetist in 1994 and was keen to learn more about the many unresolved problems of pain in our society. I subsequently went on to complete my training in pain medicine and have gone on to work in that area of specialist practice.

For me it was fascinating to see how the events of Lynda's healing flowed very much from the teaching and conceptual framework provided by Peter Horrobin. Peter outlined the multi-layered nature of our being as body, mind and spirit. He also taught about the potential role of the demonic in the spirit realm. He spoke, and I felt convicted, about the undoubted skill of Western medicine in repairing the physical after trauma but the neglect of mind and spirit which are metaphorically often left battered and bruised at the roadside. Such woundedness of mind and spirit could then impact physical state and impede the process of healing.

As I heard Lynda's story unfold there were many similarities to the life stories of those coming for help at a pain management center; the sense of being trapped in the pain with no means of escape; the emotional toll; the impact on work, family and friendships; the downward spiral of over-reliance on medication with increasing side effects. These were all familiar to me.

However, the approach to treatment demonstrated by Peter and Fiona Horrobin was anything but familiar.

Lynda was in the center of the room with Peter and Fiona kneeling beside her. She appeared to be in a trance-like state. At one level she was reliving the events of the trauma three years before and yet at another level she was held by the support of those around her in the present moment. She could both observe and recount the events of the trauma and yet also respond to the questions and prayers of Peter and Fiona. There was a vulnerability in that state, an openness, a trust, an expectation, a willingness to allow light into dark places, a desire to heal.

As I think back to that Wednesday evening and the follow-on Thursday session there were a number of issues that particularly imprinted themselves on my memory. I remember the "directed" nature of the intuitive approach that Peter and Fiona employed. A very precise process occurred that gently but firmly touched upon many aspects of Lynda's life including her generational lines. The process was full of love and a quiet confidence and trust, a faith that all would be well. Thoughts and emotions previously suppressed came to consciousness. The dimension of spirit was explored with the process including discernment of and deliverance from demonic forces. There was a very physical component, "the angelic physiotherapy," as her body moved through a remarkable range of postures that were beyond her normal capabilities.

There was an interesting segment relating to various medications that Lynda had been prescribed. The over-reliance and the side effects were linked, beyond Lynda's conscious thoughts and expectations, to the dimension of spirit and surrounding demonic activity. At one point Peter asked for my medical input as an anesthetist in regard to specifically naming drugs likely to have been used in anesthetics that Lynda had been given for a number of minor procedures after the accident. As various drugs including nitrous oxide and volatile anesthetic gases were named, Lynda lapsed transiently into a state of reduced consciousness. This led to prayer responses from Peter and Fiona that targeted demonic attachment to such drugs. My interpretation was that although there are some obvious advantages to the use of modern anesthetics and medications there can also be significant disadvantages. These include the potential for negative spiritual influence at various levels. At a corporate level attitudes such as greed within the pharmaceutical industry can have an impact. At the level of the mind, giving excessive power to the hope of an external medication-based solution can create vulnerability. At the neurobiological level there can be specific problems relating to the actions of drugs within the central nervous system.

Overwhelmingly though, as I think back, I remember the joy evident within Lynda as she came through to healing and the excitement and sense of amazement that spread throughout all as we were privileged to observe and be part of her remarkable journey.

What was extraordinary about that day was that I had so many people come up to me and tell me the most amazing stories of ways in which God had been working in their own lives while He had been ministering to me the evening before. So although the main ministry had focused on me, God had been supernaturally pouring out His healing and grace on many of those who were there. I have never known such an outpouring of God's Spirit in a single meeting before or since that night. I was just so blessed to have been a part of it and to have had so many people share their stories with me of what He did with them too.

Chapter 8

WALKING OUT MY HEALING

It was so amazing to come home and be able to tell Mum and Dad that Jesus had healed me. They had walked through the valley with me. What a joy it was for us all to share in Jesus' amazing healing! Straight after my healing I had phoned to tell them what had happened but it wasn't until they saw me for themselves that the miracle really struck home. Dad says that as soon as he saw me walk in the door, he knew that I wasn't the same girl as the one who had left four days before. Of course, they wanted to know every detail of what had happened to me. I didn't know where to start. I told them that to fully understand what had happened, they needed to listen to the teaching that had been given on the conference. So every day Mum, Dad and I listened our way through the teaching tapes of Peter Horrobin – sixteen tapes in all. That was the first time Dad had ever listened to Christian teaching tapes. My healing was a turning point particularly in Dad's Christian faith. My parents had both grown up in families that loved God and they had actually met at the Methodist church they both attended. They had been members of the Uniting Church in our local town of Bathurst and faith had been an important part of our family life together. Mum had been to a couple of Vineyard conferences with me in Sydney and was very receptive to the teaching that Jesus heals today. Mum and I were also now attending the Bathurst Christian Outreach Center where people were more open to this sort of teaching. But for Dad the idea that God still heals today was totally new and it made a great impact on his life. He had been a wonderful father in almost every way but, as he himself would now admit, had failed to exercise his role as spiritual leader of our family. My healing proved to be a catalyst, helping him to mature in his faith and move into his rightful place. Before my healing I had thought that it would be too late for a man in his mid-sixties to change. But change he did and he has never looked back!

I've asked Mum, as the person who knows me best, to describe what she saw and how she felt when I returned home:

> Before Lynda's accident in 1994 I remember her as a happy, enthusiastic and competent young lady, full of life and throwing herself into all she put her hand to. After the accident the light and life went out of her eyes. It was so hard as a mother to see her in ongoing physical and emotional pain, unable to work and wondering what the future now held for her. Lynda had always loved Jesus and really did cling to Him through those dark days. After her healing the light returned into her eyes and she was bubbling with life. We were so happy! Physically she was able to do things she could not have done before. We had our "little girl" back – all praise to God!

A couple of weeks after I had been healed, my best friend Inge was getting married, on 28 September, and I was to be her chief bridesmaid. We had been friends since High School days. She had moved into our area in her teens and had been quite lonely when she first started school. Since I was also a quiet, rather lonely girl at the time, we gravitated towards each other and gradually became friends. Inge was from a non-Christian home and was a great believer in the power of science, which resulted in some lengthy debates about Christianity between the two of us. I was absolutely thrilled when, by God's grace, in our senior years at High School Inge came to faith in Jesus. Her conversion occurred at a time when I was finding it a bit of a struggle to live as a Christian and the dramatic change in her really inspired my faith. Our friendship continued when we both studied nursing together at Charles Sturt University in Bathurst, and she had been a great support to me in the years after the accident.

Inge and her fiancé Phil had chosen to have an outdoor wedding in a park. Our main concern prior to my healing had been whether, with the back pain I had, I would be able to stand up for the ceremony. In God's amazing grace He healed me ten days before the wedding! I phoned Inge to tell her what had happened, and she was so happy for me. She later told me she could hear the life and spark back in my voice, which had been gone for the previous few years. I went to the wedding and had a great time. I didn't have any problems standing for a long period!

My healing had been one of those rare mountain-top experiences in life. Gradually I had to come down from the mountain-top and learn how to walk out my healing. One thing I did which I would advise other people to be very cautious about doing is that I stopped taking all the medications I was on. I did this because I definitely knew that God had healed me. My healing had been very dramatic and its authenticity had been confirmed. I have seen Christians stop their medications as a step of faith after having someone pray for them for healing in church. I do not believe this is the right thing to do as it may have very harmful side effects. The regular medications I was taking at the time were Zoton (for my stomach) and Tofranil (for pain; I also took other pain killers as I needed them). Jesus had done such a clear work of healing in my esophagus and stomach that I thought I would try going off the Zoton and see what happened. Nothing happened! Even without the medication I didn't have stomach pain or back pain, and the headaches had gone too. So I continued life medication free! It was a further confirmation of my healing.

The basic principle that I used to walk in the healing that Jesus had given me was to do things I would not have previously been able to do. That is not necessarily easy. In John 5:6 Jesus says to the man at the pool of Bethesda, "Do you want to get well?" This

seems a silly question for Jesus to ask a man with a long-term disability, but in that situation you get used to not being able to do
things and you get used to being disabled; you get used to not
being able to work and being dependent on others to support
you. For me it had only been two and a half years, but it really
became a part of my thinking: "I can't do that, because...," "I
would like to come, but...." and "I would like to work, but..."
In the case of the man by the pool of Bethesda Jesus cut right to
the core of the issue. It would have been easier for him to have
stayed disabled – it was his life and all he knew. It took great
courage for this man to stand and take up his mat. He was walking away from everything that was familiar to him.

It was the same for me: as I "took up my mat and walked"
I also needed great courage. I began the process of having my
mind and thinking renewed. I had to start saying, "I can do this."
I had to face my own fear of pain, even the fear of failure. Not
long after the healing I remember going to our local pool with
some friends. There was a big waterslide at the pool, which you
could go on in half-hour slots. Someone suggested that we all
went on it for half an hour. The issue for me was having to climb
the very steep stairs to the top of the waterslide over and over
again for half an hour. I had to decide between fear and faith. I
chose faith in Jesus. So I did it and had a fantastic time! I would
never have been able to do that before the healing. I came away
from the pool that day having had a great victory in my own
spirit, soul and body.

There were times too when Satan was contending for my
healing and I would have a reoccurrence of headaches or bad
back pain. At those times my gritty determination came through,
because I was not going to let Satan make me sick again and go
back to where I was before the healing. I would start praying
and tell my body to come into line with my own spirit and soul
(which were healed) and with the Spirit of God who said I was
healed and I would command the pain to go. It always went! But
I had to tough it out through those times, because each time the
pain would come it had fear attached to it – what if the pain is
here to stay? Every time this happened I would declare out loud,

"I have been healed in Jesus' name and I hold on to that healing now!" I did not need to pray for healing again – I had already received it.

As the weeks passed and I was walking out my healing with amazing victory, I was challenged about what to do with the pension I was receiving. It was called a Disability Support Pension, but I was no longer "disabled"! So I asked the Lord what He would have me do. He said three very plain words to me, "Cease the pension." I knew in my heart it was the right thing to do, but it is much easier receiving a welfare payment than it is working. I went to see the local Department of Social Security which was responsible for my pension and explained to the officer that I wanted to cancel my Disability Support Pension because I did not need it any more. I can still see the confused expression on the officer's face. Nobody ever canceled a Disability Support Pension! She had to go off and get the manager because she did not know how to handle a situation like this. I was sure they were thinking that I must have been receiving the pension because I had a mental illness. Reluctantly they let me sign it off and I expressed my appreciation for all the payments they had given me while I was on the pension. I walked out that door and took a deep breath. God had not told me He was now going to rain money out of the sky to support me. I had to go and get more work!

I was still working at the doctor's surgery ten hours a week, but since I could not get any more work there, I went and put my name down to do District Nursing – a form of nursing care provided in people's own homes. I did the orientation for it and my name was added to the casual list of Registered Nurses. I took as many shifts as I was offered. It was mainly manual work, helping elderly people with their bathing, administering medications, wound care management and the like. Many weeks between the two jobs I was working something like forty hours. Before I was healed I could not work any more than ten hours because of the fatigue, but here I was doing forty hours of hard work! That is why Jesus said to the man at the pool of Bethesda, "Do you want to get well?" The healing was free, but it was very costly!

The next major challenge I had was what I should do about
the upcoming court case. Over that year my solicitor had put
together our case and we were just about ready to go to court.
Again I prayed about it. This time I did not get a clear answer as
I did when I asked the Lord about the pension. I really felt that
God was giving me a choice, and that He would be with me in
whatever I chose.

As I considered my two options, one thing stood out to me.
It had been a very long journey for me to come to forgive the
leaders of the Mission Training School for making us do the hike
on the night I fell. That forgiveness was absolutely central to
my healing. I was now wanting to walk in that forgiveness in
my heart and the healing in my body. My concern was that if I
proceeded with the court case I might have had a strong tempta-
tion to move back to unforgiveness, which I did not want to do.
Potentially I could lose my healing.

On the other hand, I considered all I had lost as a result of
the accident. I had lost my health, having been in constant pain
and crippled by fatigue for two and a half years. I had lost a
lot of money, having been unable to resume full-time nursing
work after the training school finished. I had lived on a very low
income and been unable at times to get the medical treatment
I needed. Perhaps the worst thing that I had lost was my peace
and the joy of living. All of it had affected my relationship with
Jesus and my relationships with family and friends.

I had every right to take those responsible to court and receive
compensation. They may well have tried to deny their liability,
but it was those two leaders who made us do the hike that night
in dangerous conditions, with limited equipment, inadequate
supervision and with no training. It was me, not them, who had
suffered from pain day and night.

But by the amazing grace of God I had been healed! In front
of 150 people I had had the most extraordinary encounter with
Jesus Christ, which had totally changed my life. So I decided to
do what I thought was right: I chose to show mercy, undeserved
as it was, and drop the litigation claim!

I went to see the solicitor who was acting on my behalf and told him about how I had been healed. He was very happy for me. I said that, as a result of the healing, I wanted to drop the litigation claim. The following week I received a letter from Kenny Spring Solicitors itemizing the costs incurred in preparing the case to that point. As it was just about ready for court there were a lot of things that needed paying for! I had had a sum of money in mind that it might cost me to drop the case. It was actually three and a half times higher than what I had been anticipating! Graciously the solicitor had reduced the amount as much as he could due to my situation. But I still gulped. Even though I had been healed I still did not have hardly any money.

Soon after the letter arrived, I was in the shower one day, grumbling to God about the huge sum of money that I would need to come up with, when Father God spoke to me as clear as day. He said, "Mercy never comes cheap. It cost Jesus His life!" Wow! I apologized for grumbling and from that day I chose to walk in mercy. I knew I had done the right thing.

I made an arrangement with Kenny Spring Solicitors to pay them fortnightly whatever I could manage until the debt was paid. Each time I walked to the office to make a payment I would pray over the money and say "I am sowing mercy," because Jesus said, "Blessed are the merciful, for they will be shown mercy" (Matthew 5:7). That was an important part of walking out my healing.

The flip side of choosing to drop the litigation claim was that I was putting my complete trust in God to deal with the injustice of what had happened to me. My responsibility was to walk in forgiveness and mercy, but it was up to God to vindicate me. Sometimes when I speak to people who are in the same situation of wanting to show mercy to someone, they either want the person who has wronged them to be sorry for what they did or they want them to suffer for what they did. That is not it. I asked my solicitor to send a written copy of my testimony of how I was healed to the solicitors acting for the leaders from the Mission Training School. To this day I have never received any kind of acknowledgment or thanks. Mercy is not dependent on a response from those you are showing mercy to. They may not even care, or they may not think they did anything wrong. It took me eighteen months to pay my debt to the solicitors and no one ever said thanks. I did it for the love of Jesus, showing mercy even as He showed mercy to me. I completely took my hands off the injustice of it, trusting my Heavenly Father to deal with anything that needed dealing with. As I walked in mercy, my peace returned and multiplied.

I used to wonder about how, when He was raised from the dead after the crucifixion, Jesus bore the scars in His hands, feet and side (John 20:20). Now I understand it. I bear three scars from the accident – one on my forehead, one on my right forearm and one where I broke my right elbow. They serve as a gentle but ever-present reminder of what I went through and of God's amazing grace in saving me. As I write today it is the sixteenth anniversary of the accident. Every year for the rest of my life the 16th of April will always be special to me. It is a bit like celebrating Good Friday. I remember the suffering – I could never forget it. You cannot have the resurrection without the cross. For without the suffering I went through my healing on 18 September would never have come. More importantly, without Jesus' suffering on the cross my healing would never have come.

Chapter 9

LIVING LIFE TO THE FULL!

I know a lot of people around the world have heard about my healing through Ellel Ministries. But my healing was not the end of the story – it was an amazing chapter that took me into the next part of my life.

Jesus had given me my life back again and the world was full of exciting opportunities. One such opportunity came in August of 1997 when I had a phone call from Health Care In Christ, saying that the M/V *Doulos* (a Christian mission ship run by an international organization called Operation Mobilisation) was in Australia and they urgently needed a Christian nurse for a short term. Would I be interested in doing it? I arranged some leave with Dr Gilroy and flew to a city named Townsville in northern Australia, where I joined the ship. Here I worked full time in the clinic, helping the doctor care for the health of the 300 or so crew and staff aboard. It was fantastic.

As well as meeting so many interesting people from all over the world, I was also able to be involved in some of Operation Mobilisation's outreaches when we were in port. We traveled to Cairns on Australia's Great Barrier Reef and then to the city of Darwin in the very north of Australia. There I was able to go on a mission outreach to a small Aboriginal community on Elcho Island. It was a very memorable trip for me as it coincided with the first anniversary of my healing. I remember getting up to speak and telling the community there about the accident and how Jesus had healed me exactly one year before. My life had changed so dramatically in that year, with no further health problems, medications or fatigue. It was an incredible confirmation of my healing.

I continued with the ship when it sailed to Singapore and then Penang in Malaysia. I had never imagined I would be doing anything like this – shopping on the streets of Penang, riding around from place to place in a rickshaw and going swimming at a beach resort. My friends and I had so much fun and we laughed and laughed. It was also a privilege to be able to share the message of salvation through Jesus Christ in another culture. The ship provided a unique opportunity to cut across culture and reach out with God's love.

In December 1997 Ellel Ministries with Peter and Fiona Horrobin returned to Australia with a bigger team to hold a series of conferences. They were responding to a huge groundswell of support which was growing around Australia, partly as a result of my healing, to have an Ellel training center here. In order to equip leaders for such a training and ministry center, they were encouraging as many Australians as could manage it to come to the training schools that at that time were being held in England and Canada. They wanted to train Australians to minister in Australia, as was their heart for each nation.

I attended the Sydney conference with my mum and my pastors, Peter and Alexandra Mann. At the conference everyone had heard about the amazing healing miracle that had occurred the previous year with this girl named Lynda who had fallen off a cliff and they came wanting to know if it was real. In one session Peter gave me the opportunity to come to the platform and speak about what had happened when I was healed and in the year that followed. Everyone was gripped by the teaching of Ellel and amazed by my story.

During that conference Peter suggested to me that I might like to come to Ellel's next nine-week training school which was starting the following month in Canada. The thought of it was very exciting, but seemingly impossible. I was still in the process of paying off the solicitor and did not know how I could afford such a trip. After speaking with the Director of the Canadian training school Mum also became very keen. I prayed about it and asked God if He would provide for me. A few weeks later Mum and I were sitting on a plane crossing the Rocky Mountains, shaking our heads at the amazing provision of God for us to go to this nine-week training school together.

What I learned at the training school changed my life. God used it to show me principles to live by, covering every aspect of life. I have not gone on to be deeply involved in ministering to broken people as some do – and as my mum has –, but it gave me the most wonderful foundation for my life that has helped me through everything I have been through since that time. It also helped me become much more effective both in my own personal prayer life and also how I pray for other people. I can thoroughly recommend it.

Over the course of the training school I had one more time of ministry with Peter Horrobin. As we talked one day Peter realized that they had ministered to me from the time when I was at the bottom of the cliff, but they had not covered the time when I was at the top of the cliff. As Peter started to pray for me again, Jesus took me into the suppressed fear and dread I had felt during the hike and then the terror as my foot slipped, knowing I was falling into the unknown. I had blacked out as I started to fall, but of course my spirit had still been aware of everything that was happening. That was another part of God's mercy and love for me, as He set me free from the spirits of fear that had been at work during the accident.

One of the highlights of our stay in Canada was that Mum and I were able to go and visit Niagara Falls. It was a very cold day, in the middle of the Canadian winter, but as I looked out across the huge force of water pouring over the Falls, the most beautiful rainbow formed through the mist. I will never forget it. God had been so faithful to me and blessed Mum and me so much.

We returned to Australia full of joy and enthusiasm, wanting to practice what we had learned. Just before I left Canada,

Peter invited me to consider coming to work on the team at Ellel Pierrepont, the International Training School for Ellel Ministries, in Surrey in England. Life had certainly changed. I was a living testimony of the power and love of God to transform a life from the inside out.

A move to England required some preparation. Apart from practical considerations like getting a work visa and arranging tickets, I also had to finalize some personal matters, the most pressing of which was my outstanding debt to the solicitors' firm. I decided I should not leave the country indefinitely until I had paid the account out fully. So I worked as much as I could and, with some help from my family, I paid the debt! The debt of mercy. I was so happy when I took the last payment in.

In May 1998 I boarded a small plane in Bathurst bound for Sydney, watched by all my family. Waving them goodbye was so hard, knowing I was going to the other side of the world for an indefinite time. I flew on to London and was picked up by one of the Ellel team and driven on to Pierrepont, where Jill Southern is the Director. I already knew Jill from the first conference in Sydney. I was given a job working in the office responsible for course bookings, which I really enjoyed.

One of the highlights of my time in England was speaking at the international Ellel conference at Bournemouth attended by around a thousand people. I felt really honored to share what God had done in my life. I had never spoken to so many people before but I really enjoyed being a part of it.

I also had the opportunity to join a team led by Peter and Fiona ministering at a church conference in Slemmestad, Norway. We had an amazing time, not least because our Norwegian hosts looked after us so well. After the conference I stayed on in Norway for a few extra days for a short holiday, partly to visit a friend I'd met on the M/V *Doulos* who lived in Oslo. I have always loved mountains, and I really wanted to see some of the mountains in Norway, so one day I went for a train ride by myself to a place called Myrdal. This train ride, which connected with the Flam scenic railway, was very beautiful. When I got off the train I was in the middle of my dream picture – the mountains, the fjord, the lush green grass interspersed with beautiful wild flowers. It was magnificent. It was a time when I felt that God knew my deep unspoken dreams and He had taken me there to show me that He knew and that He loved me.

In spite of all the wonderful opportunities I was having with Ellel in England, I really missed home, and I decided I wanted to return to Australia. God had used my time in England to bring me to a deep acceptance of myself and who He had made me to be. I did not have the money for the airfare, but graciously my Aunty Mavis paid for my flight as a gift to me. So often we can think that life will always be better somewhere else. God was bringing me back to my home town of Bathurst and challenging me to be at peace with it.

At the beginning of 1997 (a few months after my healing) Diane Watson, my room-mate at the conference at which I was healed, had been the first student at the very first six-month training school at Ellel Pierrepont. Subsequently God gave Diane a vision of a magnificent property named "Gilbulla" on the outskirts of Sydney, owned at the time by the Anglican Church, being used as an Ellel ministry center, and in 2003 Ellel Australia was officially opened there, with Diane the first Center Director of Ellel Ministries in Australia.

In some way my healing was instrumental in Ellel Australia being birthed! Isn't God amazing! Now there are two centers in Australia – Ellel Gilbulla and Ellel Springhill (in Western Australia). Diane is the Center Director of Ellel Springhill and her husband Paul is the Regional Director of Ellel Ministries in Australia/Pacific and the Indian subcontinent! Mum is also a fully trained Prayer Minister at Ellel Gilbulla, and loves working as a part of the team there, counseling on healing retreats and attending various training courses.

Chapter 10

My Dream Came True

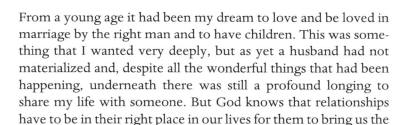

From a young age it had been my dream to love and be loved in marriage by the right man and to have children. This was something that I wanted very deeply, but as yet a husband had not materialized and, despite all the wonderful things that had been happening, underneath there was still a profound longing to share my life with someone. But God knows that relationships have to be in their right place in our lives for them to bring us the fulfillment that we seek from them.

Over an extended period of time God had been teaching me a lot about relationships. For several years I knew that He wanted me to remain single, as a deliberate decision. God wanted me to put Him in His rightful place as Number One in my life. I needed to get my priorities straight. At the time when I heard God say this to me – just two days before my accident – it had not been an easy word to accept. However, if I was really honest with myself, I knew that at that time in my life I could have loved a man more than I loved God and I knew this was not the way it should be. God wanted me to love Him most. I did not know how long this period would last or even if I would ever marry.

Over those years I had to change my way of thinking and start to love God with all my heart and be thankful for and embrace my singleness. I started to choose consciously to love

God first and foremost and I asked Him to change me where He knew I needed to change. One of the things God challenged me to do early on was to lay down my "right" to be married. We do not have the right to be married, although we may think we do. It is hard when everyone around us seems to move into marriage so easily and we are sitting on the sideline, wishing such joy would come our way. I had to lay down the dream of marriage and a family, knowing I may never receive it back.

In being willing to do so, I discovered the joy of letting God love me. Jesus Himself became like my husband and I found increasingly that He was meeting my needs. I talked to Him about everything and spent active time listening to Him. Sometimes I would just sit and listen to music with Him. Other times I would go for a walk on our farm and enjoy the beauty of nature with Him. Sometimes He gave me a Scripture to lead or encourage me, or sometimes an impression. There were always times when there was nothing at all. But as I started to taste His love, it became the only thing that would truly satisfy me. It did not matter if He did not speak to me; I would just come back next time and wait until He would refresh my heart again. I started to find Jesus bringing me deep contentment and peace.

I was also challenged to consider what a godly relationship in a marriage would be like. I determined my responsibility was to come to the relationship to give, not to take. My needs should be continually met in Jesus, so that I could give into the relationship. It was not about me and my needs being fulfilled. It was all about a life of sacrifice for the love of the other, giving when you have nothing left to give. So I started preparing myself by learning to let Jesus meet my needs.

This period of enforced singleness by God had eventually come to an end. I can remember the day very clearly when, as I was seeking God in prayer, He told me that the discipline of singleness which He had put me under had now ended and from that time He was giving me the choice of whether I wanted to be single or to marry. I had become so content with being single, with Jesus as my best friend, that it was then not an easy decision

The early years

Lynda as a little girl leaving the farm and going to church.

On the farm: Lynda, Dad (Don), Owen (brother) and Robyn (sister).

Lynda with grandparents and brother in front of their home in Queenscliff.

Queenscliff beach mission where Lynda asked Jesus to become her 'special friend'.

Lynda's graduation from university as a registered nurse, celebrated with her family.
FRONT: Lynda's mother and her Nanna, Lynda and Robyn. BACK: Owen and Lynda's father.

The accident & the healing

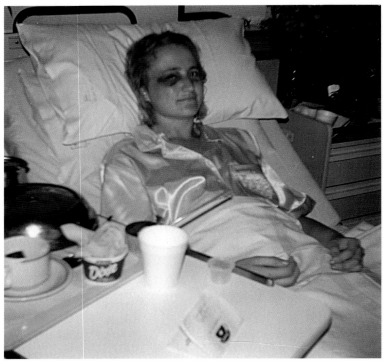

Lynda in hospital three days after the accident.

Sydney Ellel conference, December 1997 (a year after the healing): Peter Horrobin, Lynda's mother Joan, Lynda and Fiona Horrobin

Life after healing

Going back to her farming roots, Lynda rounded up cattle with her father.

Just ten days after her healing Lynda (left) looks full of life at her best friend Inge's wedding.

Paul & Diane Watson.
Paul is now Ellel Ministres Regional Director of Australia Pacific and the Indian Sub Continent. Diane is Center Director for Ellel Ministries Australia (Springhill, Perth).

At the opening of Ellel Ministries Gilbulla: Peter Horrobin together with Lynda and her father, mother and husband Leigh.

Ellel Ministries' first Center in Australia: Ellel Gilbulla, near Sydney. There is a second center at Springhill, Perth.

The present day: walking in wholeness & healing

Lynda at home on the family farm, Australia.

FRONT: Kirilee, Izaak and Laura. BACK: Leigh and Lynda

The gift of children

Laura & Kirilee

Kirilee

Izaak

Izaak & Lynda

Beautiful Jasmyn

Lynda with Jasmyn

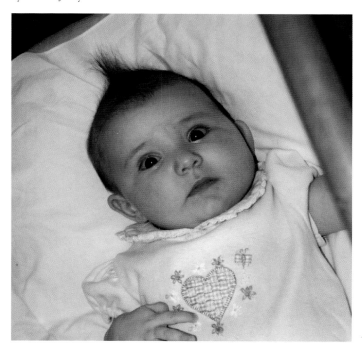

Leigh & Lynda

to make but over time I chose marriage and knew when the time was right He would honor that choice.

A powerful experience I had during my time on the M/V *Doulos* had confirmed me in my choice. One evening when we were out at sea, near the Gulf of Carpentaria, I was sitting in my favorite spot on the bow of the ship and, looking out over the wide expanse of the ocean, praying on my own. As I prayed, I heard God speak to me along similar lines to the way He had spoken to Abraham many centuries before (see Genesis 17). I heard my Heavenly Father call me "Mother." He then told me to look at the stars in the sky and to believe Him for a husband and for children. This was a step of faith, because there were no men on the horizon of my life at that time. But I believed God. I had no idea of who or how or when. This was the first promise God gave me about having a family, and when God gives you a promise you receive it and hold onto it with everything you have. In that moment, as I looked up to a beautiful, clear sky full of stars, I trusted that somehow He was going to bring it to pass. This was to be the next part of my journey, but before then I had to learn another important lesson about living as God's child, and that was the lesson of waiting! God does not march to the beat of our drum. He is God and we have to let Him orchestrate His miracles in our lives in His time. It is always worth the wait!

By now it was 2001, and for the last year I had been working for a company called Southern Cross Community Healthcare, which provided a range of nursing and community healthcare services. As the Care Coordinator I was responsible for overseeing all our services in the local area. A lot of the people we cared for were elderly, and I had to visit them regularly in their homes, initially to assess their needs and then to make sure everything was working well and they were happy with our services. I enjoyed my work with Southern Cross, but I was coming to a crossroads and needed to make a decision about whether to continue with them or move on to something else. I remember one day as I was driving around with my work, I said to God, "What do You want me to do?"

Now at the time Ellel was just preparing to open a center in Australia and I would have been more than happy to go and work on the team. There was also a possibility of going to work with Jews in Eastern Europe, which I would have been equally happy to do as I had long held a heart for Israel as a Christian and I was keen to do anything I could to bless the Jewish people. I was ready to go wherever God said. I will always remember exactly where I was in the car when God gave me His reply: "Stay with Southern Cross"! I was surprised more than anything. Here I was ready to serve Him anywhere in the world and He wanted me to stay right where I was. So I trusted Him.

The following month Southern Cross received a new referral to a man who required nursing care as a result of a stroke. His name was Charles Scott, or Mac for short. I drove out to the farm and was instantly drawn to the beautiful garden and the great atmosphere around the sheds. I met Mac and his wife Maisie and his son Leigh, who had been caring for Mac at home since he had suffered a major stroke a few years previously. I experienced such lovely country hospitality as I undertook my assessment. Mac had been farming all of his life, and Leigh had continued his passion for the land and ran the property with beef cows.

I remember being struck on that first visit by the complete love and dedication that Maisie and Leigh must have for Mac to be caring for him at home with such severe disabilities. He was fully paralyzed down one side of his body and needed a wheelchair. His speech was also badly impaired. But Leigh had rigged up a ramp so that he could take him around the farm each day in the farm ute.* He even managed to get Mac up into the cattle truck so he could go to a cattle sale with him. I had never in my nursing career seen someone so dependent following a stroke cared for in their own home so well. It was a situation of great love, respect and sacrifice that is rarely seen and it intrigued me. Leigh walked me out to the car and asked me if I would like to

---

* Short for "utility vehicle," a car/truck hybrid.

come over on a day off and look around the farm. Having only just met the family and wanting to maintain a professional relationship, I declined.

I continued my routine visits to Mac over the coming few months and always enjoyed them. Leigh always seemed to be there whenever I came and on one more occasion he asked me over, which I again declined. On another visit, however, he was not there as he was at a bull sale and I had a lovely talk with Maisie. As Maisie and I walked out to the car, she said to me that Leigh really wanted to know if I was married! Only a mother could say something like that! I told her I was not and she could tell Leigh that. It was then for the first time that I started to wonder if Leigh could be the man that God had for me. I also knew that on my next visit Leigh would be there and that he would ask me out again. And he did. Having had two knockbacks for asking me over to the farm, this time he tried a different approach and asked me out for dinner. I told him I would love to see the farm with him, and that I would be over on Saturday at 2 o'clock!

I drove down the driveway at 2 o'clock on Saturday. This was our first date. Leigh had the ute and two motorbikes sitting out. He asked me how I wanted to go around the farm. On the motorbikes, of course! I jumped on a red motorbike, started it up and started driving down the road to go and see the farm. Leigh got such a surprise to see me handle the motorbike so well that he was left standing and had to try and catch me up. I still remember that I was wearing my old hiking boots that I had fallen off the cliff with.

The farm was absolutely beautiful. We saw all the different breeds of crossbred cows and I had fun trying to guess what they were. The main breed was Angus/Hereford cross cows, which Leigh crossed with Limousin or Charolais bulls. There were certainly a few paddocks that Leigh described as "mixed grills" because of the mixture of breeds there. Leigh and his father had also run sheep over the years and Leigh ran his own pig operation. The farm had been in his father's family since the 1840s. I had never felt so alive as I did that day riding around the farm with Leigh. He was the perfect gentleman and opened and closed every gate for me. Near the end of the ride, as the evening approached and it was getting cold, we were riding down a hill and Leigh's motorbike was in front of me. As I looked across at him I wondered again if Leigh was the man that God had for me. It all seemed so amazing.

After that first bike ride we did go out for dinner. As I was getting in the car to leave that evening Leigh asked if he could ring me on Tuesday night. He rang and we arranged to meet in Bathurst the following day for lunch. That was the beginning of an amazing journey. I talked to Southern Cross about me seeing Leigh, not wanting to have a professional/personal conflict. My boss did not see any difficulty in Southern Cross continuing to provide Mac's nursing care.

I had been so aware over the years of my Heavenly Father's hand in protecting me from the wrong men for me. Leigh had been so forthright and the only man who had ever been like that with me. I mainly wanted to know if this was God's will and, if it were, whether Leigh himself was thinking of marriage. I do not believe in couples just dating for dating's sake. I had been waiting on God's timing and for the right man. I was now in the process of determining if Leigh was that man – I was not going to settle for anything less than God's best for me.

We talked a lot in those early weeks as we were getting to know each other and did lots of things together. We went for lots of drives and saw so much beautiful country. One day we went to a local house church together, as I had been invited to share the testimony of my healing. After the service we stopped by a lake and were talking together when Leigh asked me to marry him! It had all happened so quickly. All his family and friends had thought that Leigh, who was a little bit older than me, was a confirmed bachelor, but he too had been waiting for the right person. He told me that on the first day he met me he knew I was the one he would marry. It really was love at first sight! Isn't God amazing? I could imagine God laughing and smiling as His plan for me unfolded. The following week I replied and said I would marry him. That was really the start of our courtship.

We didn't tell anyone immediately as we wanted to continue the process of getting to know each other. We talked about God, my accident and healing, and the prospect of having a family. We dreamed of what our life would be together. Leigh told me that as he was praying one day, God had told him that I had "crossed a few dry creeks." He told me that I was not to worry any more because he was going to look after me and provide for me. The description of the "few dry creeks" was very accurate. Bit by bit we started to love each other and trust each other.

Two months after Leigh had asked me to marry him, Mum and Dad were going up to Queensland in the north of Australia for a holiday and asked me to come along. We also invited Leigh to join us for whatever time he could get away. Leigh and I both thought that this might be a good opportunity to talk to Dad about us getting engaged. I wondered whether Leigh would actually be able to get away from the farm and have a break from caring for his dad as it had been nine years since his last holiday. When I went to pick him up at the airport and saw his distinctive farmer's hat a head above everyone else I was so thrilled. He had come away from the farm for me! That confirmed to me that Leigh was totally serious about getting married and that he meant everything he had been saying to me. Leigh asked Dad that week if he gave his consent to our marriage, which he did. Mum and Dad were both so thrilled for us. To celebrate, we went out to dinner at the restaurant of the hotel where Mum and Dad had spent their honeymoon forty-two years before.

On returning home we announced our engagement and started to think about getting a house. Leigh's intention was to find a beautiful spot that we both liked on the farm and build a house on it. The thought of marrying a farmer and living on the land was just so right. My heavenly Father was fulfilling my dream as a girl growing up on our farm with my dad. We picked a location and found a builder. I had always wanted to have a home in the mountains looking across a beautiful valley. It was who God had made me to be. Leigh and God were bringing those dreams into reality, with no measure spared. At about that time I recorded in my diary something that Leigh said to me:

"My love for you is an expression of God's love for you"! Isn't that beautiful? That is how God intends marriage to be.

I spent quite a lot of time with Mac in those months when I was visiting Leigh. The two had always been very close and someone once told me that Mac had always said that there would never be a woman good enough for Leigh. So one day, in Leigh's presence, I decided to ask Mac. His speech was mainly limited to yes and no answers. I said to Mac, "I believe you've always said there was never a woman good enough for Leigh." He nodded. Then with a bit of anxiety I asked, "Am I good enough?" He said "Yes" and nodded and held my hand! That meant a great deal to both Leigh and me. I only wish that I could have known Mac more and been able to have full conversations with him.

In January of 2002 the decision was made by other members of the family that Mac should go into a nursing home. Before Mac left, Leigh and I drove him up to the hill where we were going to build our house. Leigh showed him the spot, knowing Mac knew every inch of the property, having farmed it his whole life. Leigh asked him if he thought it was a good location for a house, which he agreed it was. We told him about our wedding plans and our hope to have children. We knew we had Mac's blessing. Two months after Mac went to the nursing home he passed away. Had it not been for Mac's stroke, Leigh and I may never have met.

On 7 September 2002 my dream (and Leigh's) came true! Leigh and I were married at the Lithgow Uniting Church and I am sure all of heaven rejoiced with us. When Leigh took my hand in the wedding ceremony I knew everything would be all right. Leigh had proved his love to me beyond any doubt, and I knew he was prepared to sacrifice anything for me. I knew God was with us, and whatever was before us we would face together. We loved each other and totally committed our lives to each other. Our house was finished a few weeks after the wedding. I am so glad that I trusted God and let Him orchestrate the most amazing love story – Leigh and Lynda's love story!

Chapter 11

WHEN, GOD, WHEN?

———————————— ≈ ————————————

Given both our ages when we married – Leigh was forty-seven and I was thirty-two – we were keen to start a family as soon as we were able. The month following our marriage I became pregnant. We were both so excited. Mixed in with the excitement, I had plenty of questions as to what the experience of child-bearing was going to be like.

I had all the tests that I was recommended. At twelve weeks Leigh and I went to the hospital and saw the first ultrasound of our baby. It was amazing. Such beautiful tiny little hands and feet, kicking and moving so freely. We were not able to tell the sex of the baby at that stage, but I seemed to have an inner knowing that the baby was a boy. Leigh felt the same. Whenever he spoke to the baby, he always called him Jack.

When Jack was fifteen weeks, I went to the toilet at home and had a small knob of tissue come away. There was no blood or anything like that, but I was still concerned. I phoned Leigh, who was at a cattle sale, and asked him to come home. We contacted our doctor who recommended the best thing to do was to have an ultrasound to check what was happening. The mood was very somber in the ultrasound room. All I wanted to know was whether the baby was all right. Finally the sonographer told me that she could not find a heartbeat. Our Jack had died!

I was admitted to the hospital. Although Jack had died, he was still inside my womb. The doctor decided to take me into the operating theater the following morning. Leigh stayed at the hospital with me until late that night. Even though we were told how common miscarriages are – up to one in four pregnancies – that did not change the fact that we had lost our first son. I felt as if I had failed Leigh. Not long before Leigh had to go I started to vomit. I vomited and vomited. That was the start of the worst night of my life. My body was going into labor, but never having been pregnant before I did not really understand what was happening. Maybe the nurses monitoring me thought I knew, but I was in such distress that I had no capacity to think through what was happening. There was so much blood that by the middle of that night I thought I was going to die. Even when I fell off the cliff it did not once occur to me that I might die. Never have I felt the presence of death so close to me, and it was horrible. When I saw the sunrise alighting on the window, I was so deeply relieved. I knew I would live.

Early that morning the nurse brought my little Jack in to me in a small basket. Without ever being consciously aware of it, I had delivered him whole during the night. Nobody had told me. The nurse confirmed to me what I had known – the baby was a boy. She left me to spend some time with Jack's little body. I had only just got used to the idea of having a baby, and now he was gone. I spent my time loving and talking to him and then saying goodbye. I trusted him into Jesus' hands, knowing my son was in heaven with Him. Jack's birthday was the 9th of January 2003.

I went to the operating theater later that morning to have a D and C. Although I was relieved to go home, I felt so empty and disappointed. I had a pervading sense of failure. Fortunately we were able to take Jack's body home with us, and Leigh and I buried him at the farm on the top of the hill above our house, next to an old gum tree. Leigh carved his name into the tree with his pocket knife.

As my mum and dad sought to comfort me in those early weeks, Dad decided to tell me that a few days before Jack had died he had had a dream about Jack. Jack had been all wrapped up in a small basket and someone was carrying him. All Dad could see was his little face and dark hair. Then the person carrying the basket stopped and Jack said to Dad, "I've got to go away. I would like you to come with me and hold my hand." Dad said to Jack, "I'm sorry I can't see your hand, but I can see your ear. Will that do?" Jack said, "No, it has to be my hand...but don't worry, I will be all right." Dad could not see who was carrying the basket, but the figure slowly walked away carrying Jack.

After the initial shock and trauma I gradually came again to trust my Heavenly Father. I don't know why Jack had to go, but it was such a comfort for me to know that God had him in His hand and that he was going to be all right. I had always believed in God's love for unborn babies and that actions such as abortion really grieve His heart, but Dad's dream reinforced to me that miscarried babies really do matter to God and that God cares for unborn babies when they leave this earth. That meant so much to me. As a result of his dream Dad has always had a special bond with Jack, and often goes up to the hill to spend time at the place where he is buried. From the time I lost Jack, deep in my spirit I wanted to have another son.

Leigh and I grieved in the early weeks, but hearing how common miscarriages are, we decided to have another try at having a baby. I believed God had called me to be a mother and was going to give it everything I could. I still had a sense of failure that I wanted to erase. In June of 2003 I conceived again. I realized as I started the second pregnancy that one thing I had lost with Jack was the sheer joy and anticipation of having a baby. For most women it is a very exciting time when they are in full bloom as their baby grows in the womb. As a result of the miscarriage I was now supersensitive to my body. Every time I went to the toilet I was anxious. Every unusual twinge caused me great distress. I was tormented by fear and anxiety.

Nevertheless, everything was going along fine. I made it through the first twelve weeks, which is the usual time of miscarriage – but I had done that before, and still miscarried at fifteen weeks. I made it through the fifteen-week mark and was really relieved. I had a full ultrasound at eighteen weeks and was told that the baby was a girl. Since Leigh had not been able to get to that ultrasound with me, I came home and told him about our beautiful daughter, and he was thrilled. Sometimes as a parent you can just know instinctively what the name of a child is, as we did with Jack: our daughter's name was going to be Lily.

One evening, when I was approaching the twentieth week of my pregnancy, I went to the toilet and there seemed to be a discharge from the vagina and there was a bit of blood streaked on the toilet paper. Having only had one prior pregnancy that had ended in a miscarriage, I really did not have any idea what was happening, so I rang the doctor. He told me to come to the hospital the following morning. They sent me straight in for an ultrasound to check the baby. To my great relief there on the ultrasound screen was my Lily, moving about very happily. The ultrasound showed, however, that my cervix had opened and Lily's little foot was coming down through the opening of the cervix. This was bad. I was told that there was no hope of Lily coming through this. She was going to die. But as I looked at the ultrasound screen, I saw the most beautiful thing. Lily's body seemed to square up to the camera somehow and her right arm and hand came up next to her face and, as clear as day, she waved to me.

I needed to be transferred to another hospital and, as I rode along in the back of the hospital vehicle, my heart really sank. I cried out to God to save Lily. I could not believe that I was going to lose our second child. This was not how things were supposed to turn out. All the pain of losing Jack snowballed into this situation with Lily.

Having been admitted to a surgical ward, alongside patients undergoing surgery, I started the second worst night of my life. After visiting hours had ended and Leigh had gone home, as the long night hours stretched ahead of me I felt so alone and without any comfort. I wanted someone to tell me what was happening. Around midnight I asked to see a midwife or a doctor, but I was told they could not get one for me. I think my body was starting to go into labor again as I had pain coming and going in waves. The nurse then told me that I was just anxious because I did not know what was going to happen and she left me. I was so shocked and hurt that I should be treated so poorly. She may well have been right, but I did not think that should mean I was denied access to qualified staff who could help me through the trauma. I did not see a doctor or midwife from the time I arrived at the hospital until the following day. After the nurse's harsh words to me, I withdrew completely, unable to face any further confrontation. I knew that I was not going to receive any support that night from the staff.

I knew that Lily was still alive, so I spent my time talking to her while I still had her with me. I poured out my heart to her, having to tell her a lifetime of things in only a few hours. I told her how sorry I was that I had let her down. I told her about heaven and that her brother Jack was there. I asked her to give our love to Jack. I prayed and prayed with her, surrounding her with my love. I cried as quietly as I could as I went through the labor, since I was sharing a room with three other patients. In the middle of the night when I had said all I could say to Lily, the urgency to talk to her stopped. I knew she was gone. Mercifully I fell asleep.

The next morning I was taken to the operating theater for another D and C. As with Jack, I had delivered Lily all by myself in the middle of the night and they found her when I was in the theater. Again the nurse brought her into me in a basket. I spent more time with her than I had with Jack, just wanting to touch her and hold her. As I held Lily, her nose ran with a little fluid and I was so pleased to be able to dry her nose. At least I could do something for her. We buried Lily next to Jack and have always been comforted that they are together. Lily's birthday was 27 September 2003.

After Lily died I was really devastated. There arose a very real sense of doubt as to whether we would be able to have children. To have lost two children in our first year of marriage had been so hard. I felt a compound sense of guilt and failure. I so wanted to have children with Leigh. I also knew that I could not keep having miscarriages. It was so devastating physically,

emotionally, mentally and spiritually. Leigh and I made the decision that, to give me a break and give my body time to heal, I
should leave work. In working through his grief, Leigh found
great solace in stopping by the gum tree as he went around the
farm each day and spending time with Jack and Lily. Leigh's
strength really helped to give me strength in what was a very
difficult time for us both.

Before I could consider going through another pregnancy, I
had to hear from my heavenly Father. I needed a promise from
Him, a promise about having a child, that I could stand on no
matter what. I knew that when God makes you a promise, He
will keep it. Faithfulness is a part of the character of God. I needed
to know that God was going to give us a child.

Months before – in fact, the month after Leigh and I married – while visiting my friend Inge's church one weekend, the
Pastor, Linda Cowie, had told me about a Christian City Church
Women's Conference that she had just been to, adding quite
unexpectedly that she believed God was leading her to tell me
that I should come to it the following year. At the time I had
just fallen pregnant with Jack, so I didn't think I would be able
to make it to the conference, expecting to have recently given
birth to a baby, but I had kept what she had said to me in mind.
The conference was scheduled for 24–25 October 2003 and was
called "Women Dreaming." After what had happened and the
loss of Jack and Lily I knew that this conference was the place
for me.

Mum came with me. I was going to bang on the gates of
heaven for a promise from God about having a child. The first
day of the conference I found quite difficult emotionally because
there were a lot of women with babies or women expecting
babies. That was hard. Over the conference we talked about our
dreams and what we wanted God to do for us in our lives. I
knew my dream – to have children. On the second day, quite
unexpectedly, Pastor Chris Pringle, the hostess of the conference, said that she wanted to pray for anyone who wanted to
have children, but had not been able to. My heart started to
pound and it is the only time in my life that I have run up for

an altar call. But this was my moment, this was why I was here. Pastor Chris prayed for me, but did not give any specific words of promise. From the time I had that prayer I did, however, feel a real release from the pain of seeing babies and pregnant women and I no longer felt hurt by it. Later that day we drew pictures of our dreams in our "Dreams' Book" and brought them to God as the prayers of our heart. I drew a picture of Leigh and me with children. The leaders anointed our books with oil and prayed for our dreams to come to pass.

The day after the conference Mum and I attended the Sunday morning service at Inge's church. As I was talking to Pastor Linda, who had also been at the Women's Conference, God released His promise to me. Pastor Linda told me that when she had seen me up on the platform at the conference receiving prayer from Pastor Chris, God had shown her a Scripture. It was the story of the Shunammite woman from 2 Kings 4. Since the Shunammite woman has helped Elisha by providing food and shelter for him, the prophet calls for her and asks her what can be done for her. While she seems satisfied that she has a home among her own people, the prophet's helper Gehazi tells him that "she has no son and her husband is old." Elisha calls the Shunammite woman to come and see him a second time and, as she stands in the doorway to his room (v. 15), he gives her a promise, "About this time next year you will hold a son in your arms" (v. 16). Pastor Linda said to me that as I stood at the altar, it was as if I was standing "in the doorway" as the Shunammite woman had done, and she saw the promise of having a child being released to me as it had been to her!

As I looked at the Scripture myself, I really empathized with the Shunammite woman's reply to Elisha. "No, my lord," she objects. "Don't mislead your servant, O man of God!" (v. 16b). I understood her completely. What he was saying to her was so precious that it was better not to have the promise and not be disappointed than to believe for the prayer of your heart and have it denied. This Shunammite woman had obviously suffered greatly in waiting for her dream to come to pass. The story continues, however:

But the woman became pregnant, and the next year about
that same time she gave birth to a son, just as Elisha had
told her. (v. 17)

So God was faithful to His promise to her through Elisha and
brought her dream to pass. I dared to take hold of this promise for
me and believe that God was going to be faithful to me and give
us a child the following year. I have heard it said many times over
the years by different people that FAITH is spelt like this: RISK! It
is absolutely true. I was trusting God with everything I had and it
was nothing short of scary and exciting at the same time.

The second thing I did was to go to Ellel Ministries at Gilbulla
and have a day of prayer ministry with my friend Diane Watson
and another counselor. I needed to grieve for the loss of Jack
and Lily. We also had to pray into the trauma I had experienced
in both Jack's and Lily's birth. I had to forgive the people who
had hurt me and who had failed to support me with both births.
We prayed as well about any demonic influence that may have
affected me while I was under general anesthetic in the operating theater.

One of the most powerful points in the ministry was when
Diane prayed for the Holy Spirit to come and sever the soul-tie
between me and both Jack and Lily. They were gone and I had
to let them go, so that I could go on living my life. I had learnt
about soul-ties initially from my healing in 1996 and I knew
they could have a powerful effect. Having the soul-tie severed
between us did not mean I no longer loved Jack and Lily or
cherished them. It was the reality of having to release them into
God's loving care. Once the soul-ties were severed I felt a tre-
mendous freedom and liberty. I was not going to be held back
from my future now.

Another important element of the ministry was prayer for
God to bring a cleansing to my womb. Two babies had died in
my womb and there was a very real possibility that there may
have been a spirit of death affecting my womb. So Diane commanded any spirit of death to go, in Jesus' name. We also broke
the power of any curses that were stopping me from having

children: through any words people had spoken against us or through any curses coming down either Leigh's or my generational line. Such negative words and curses can have a major impact on couples being able to conceive and/or carry a healthy baby full term.

Then Diane laid hands upon me and prayed for God's blessing so that I would be able to bear a healthy child to full term. We prayed about every aspect of the pregnancy. I confessed my fears and asked God to help me through the next pregnancy. I left Ellel confident that God was going to be with me and that I was going to have a child as He had promised.

I believe both the receiving of the promise through the women's conference and the prayer ministry were essential to prepare me for what was ahead. I needed both.

A few months later I fell pregnant again. I was excited, but still had some apprehension. But this time I had God's promise to stand on. So every day, or as often as I needed to, I thanked God for His promise that I was going to have a child. As often as the fear came to me and tormented me that I was going to fail, I would reply with God's promise. To stand on God's promises might sound easy, but it actually took all the courage I had. During that pregnancy I used to sing worship songs about the faithfulness of God so much. I stood in the face of my fear and chose to believe God.

Another choice that Leigh and I made early in the pregnancy was to find a specialist obstetrician in Sydney. We went to meet our new doctor, wondering if he was the right person to help us. Dr Bell was very kind. He diagnosed me as having an "incompetent cervix" and indicated that when I reached about the twelve-week mark, he would admit me into hospital and insert a cervical suture to ensure that the cervix would not be able to open prematurely as it had done before. The suture was duly inserted and afterwards we saw the first ultrasound of our new baby.

One of the blessings of this pregnancy was that we got to have much more regular ultrasounds to make sure everything was OK. I loved having the ultrasounds. They were like a form of healing for me as I watched our baby kicking around and could monitor how much growth was taking place between each appointment. We became good friends with the sonographer, a beautiful lady named Tracey, and the receptionist Pat. At our eighteen-week ultrasound we found out that our baby was a girl. We did not have a name for her as quickly as we did with Jack and Lily. The baby was due at the beginning of October, which was just under a year from the time I had received God's promise that we would have our baby "about this time" the following year. Everything was on track for God being faithful.

Every week was a milestone for me as I steadily got bigger and bigger. My hope began to rise. Dr Bell was really wonderful to us. Mum and Dad were such an amazing support to me through all this time. Mum came to most of my appointments in Sydney with me and we had many lovely times together.

In September Dr Bell decided to admit me into hospital for the birth. I had gone full term and the baby was ready to be born! The suture needed to be removed in order for me to be able to proceed with a natural birth. Leigh was there with me the whole time. We had the most beautiful little girl – Kirilee Louise Scott, 7 pounds 13 ounces. And her birthday was 18 September 2004 – the eighth anniversary of the day God had healed me after the accident!!! Praise be to God! He had, indeed, continued His healing, given us the desire of our heart and proved Himself the most faithful, loving God!

Chapter 12

OUR PRINCESS

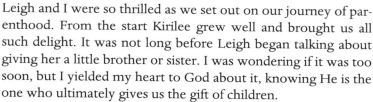

Leigh and I were so thrilled as we set out on our journey of parenthood. From the start Kirilee grew well and brought us all such delight. It was not long before Leigh began talking about giving her a little brother or sister. I was wondering if it was too soon, but I yielded my heart to God about it, knowing He is the one who ultimately gives us the gift of children.

One night when Leigh and I were in our bedroom, I felt the presence of Jesus come to our bedroom door. It is the only time it has ever happened. I did not visually see anything, but I knew Jesus was there and He waited at the door for me to invite Him in. Sometimes when Jesus speaks to me it is in very plain words or through a verse or passage from the Bible. But that night His communication with me was not so confined to words. Deep in my spirit somehow I knew that I was going to fall pregnant and have another child. He also promised me for the first time that I would have a son. By the end of that month I was indeed pregnant again, as I knew I would be.

I returned again to Dr Bell in Sydney for a repeat of the process we had gone through with Kirilee. I did not have the same level of anxiety with this pregnancy because I knew that we could do it – Kirilee was our proof. I went for my full ultrasound at nineteen weeks and found that the baby was a beautiful girl.

I was surprised at first, thinking that Jesus had promised me a son, but when I thought it through I realized that He had not specified which pregnancy the son would be. So we very happily prepared for the birth of our second daughter.

Everything went along smoothly and I felt very at peace within myself. When I reached full term Dr Bell booked me into the hospital in Sydney. I again had a wonderful natural delivery, with Leigh there supporting me. We had a beautiful daughter – Jasmyn Evelyn Scott, weighing 8 pounds 7 ounces. Jasmyn was born on 13 October 2005, the wedding anniversary of Leigh's parents. Kirilee and Jasmyn were born thirteen months apart.

We had done it again! God had been so wonderful to us and life was so good. My hands now were very full. Kirilee enjoyed getting to know her little sister and passing her toys to play with. One day Mum took the two girls for a walk in town in the double pram. As they walked along, Kirilee reached out and took Jasmyn's little hand and just held it for some time. Mum was so touched and said it was one of the most beautiful things she had ever seen.

Jasmyn was a very placid and content little girl. We took Kirilee and Jasmyn to church each week and I really enjoyed dressing them up in pretty little girls' clothes. Many of the people at church developed a special bond with both the children.

After a couple of months I still had not fully recovered from the birth and it was discovered that I had a post partum hemorrhage which required minor surgery, so in December I had to return to the hospital in Sydney. As I was still breast-feeding I took Jasmyn with me. The surgery went well, but while I was in the theater recovery room, I developed a fever and became quite ill. I was transferred to the Children's Ward, so that the nurses there could help me with Jasmyn. Leigh had stayed with me for the first days while I was in hospital but by then he had had to go home and I was alone with Jasmyn for a few days. She was the most beautiful companion. When I felt lonely I would look over at her and the loneliness would leave. It turned out to be a very special time between us.

I was able to return home just before Christmas. We shared Christmas that year with Leigh's mother and some other family members. I took the most beautiful photograph of Jasmyn lying on Leigh's knees, looking up at him with a big smile.

In mid January I was over at Mum and Dad's one day with the two girls. Just as I was wrapping Jasmyn up to put her to bed for her afternoon nap, Dad looked at her and had a very strange feeling. He told us that she looked exactly as Jack had looked in the dream that he had had just before Jack died. We were not sure what to make of it, so we put it aside.

Later that month, I was again putting Jasmyn to bed for a sleep when I had a very strong urge to pray for her. I did not know what it was particularly that I was praying about, but I just knew I needed to pray. This urge to pray for her stayed with me for a number of days, so I continued to pray for her more than usual.

My routine at that time involved me taking Kirilee and Jasmyn over to my Mum and Dad's place of a Friday morning, so I could do an exercise class and run a few errands. On Friday 3 February 2006 – a day that was to change our lives – when I got back to Mum and Dad's, Mum said that Jasmyn had been a bit unsettled, which was unusual. So I picked her up and took her up to the front hallway where I got out some lovely toys and lay down on the floor and played with her. She was laughing and playing with me. Then I took her up to the bedroom for a sleep. I gave her a cuddle and a kiss and put her into her cot.

Maybe an hour and a half later Mum and I both went into the bedroom to get her up, as I was ready to return home. I will never forget what I saw. When Mum picked Jasmyn up, her face was blue and white! She had been pressed up against the cot rails, which had caused stripes to form down her face. I was not thinking clearly. Surely this was not how it looked. Somehow Mum and I managed to agree that she go and ring for an ambulance. Being a nursing sister I was familiar with Cardio-pulmonary Resuscitation (CPR), but I had never had to do it on a real baby, let alone my own. I laid Jasmyn on the floor and started the procedure of resuscitation. I still could not process the thought that she might be dead. It was just too inconceivable.

I cried out to God and prayed for her to respond to the CPR.
I begged her to breathe. But she just lay there motionless. Then
I remember saying one thing to her from the depth of my heart,
"Please don't leave me!"

Kirilee was toddling around wondering what was happening.
Mum was on the phone calling for an ambulance, Dad was out
waiting by the car not realizing what was happening, I was doing
CPR – and little Kirilee saw it all. There was not a thing I could
do about it. Before I knew it a string of ambulances arrived followed by a helicopter. I was relieved of the CPR by one of the
ambulance officers who took over. They told me that I had done
a good job with the CPR. They then tried everything they could
to help Jasmyn breathe again.

I immediately phoned Inge to ask her to pray for Jasmyn. Inge
says she will never forget the sound of my voice that day. I tried
to explain to her what was happening, but I did not even really
know myself. I could not contact Leigh as he had been at a cattle
sale in Sydney and would have been traveling home in the truck
without a phone.

The decision was made to take Jasmyn to the hospital. They
did not let me travel with her, but took me in a separate ambulance. Things were certainly not looking good. Mum and Dad
stayed at their home to mind Kirilee. I left a message with Leigh's
brother to locate him as soon as he came in from the sale and tell
him to come to the hospital.

The medical team continued to work on Jasmyn for maybe
another hour but to no avail. Finally the doctor pronounced
Jasmyn dead. There were tubes all over her beautiful little body.
This was my little princess and she was gone.

One of the hardest things I have ever done in my life was to
face Leigh when he arrived at the hospital. He was completely
bewildered, not knowing what had happened. I told him that
Jasmyn had died, and saw the pain and shock in his face. I had
wanted to make him happy, not be the bearer of devastating
news. Recalling how happy and well Jasmyn had been that
morning before he went to the sale, he asked what had happened. I explained it as best I could, still not understanding

it myself. It was one of only two times that I have ever seen Leigh cry.

My sister Robyn came to the hospital and stayed with me, which was a comfort. Our pastors also came and prayed with us. The rest of the time was all a bit of a blur, with various people coming to see us, but I do clearly recall the time that they brought Jasmyn's little body into us, still with the tube in her mouth, for us to spend some time with her. We just held her and I did not want to let her go.

We had to talk to a police detective, who needed to rule out the possibility of foul play. Finally it was time to go home. Leigh decided to go on ahead in order to be able to talk to his mother about what had happened and spend some time with her. The hardest moment for me was when I went to leave the hospital and I had to leave Jasmyn there. It just did not seem right to walk away from her.

I went over to Mum and Dad's to pick up Kirilee. We were all in such shock. I remember feeling the pain of the empty car seat as I drove home that night. I felt so alone for some reason. There was only one person that night that I wanted to contact – Peter Horrobin. After putting Kirilee to bed, I sat up and wrote an email to Peter. The following morning Peter and Fiona phoned me up. I really needed to hear from them. I was so touched by their love and offer to have people within Ellel Ministries praying for us.

The unexplained nature of Jasmyn's death meant that a coroner's investigation was required and she had to be taken to Sydney for an autopsy. Like any mother I was grieved to think Jasmyn's perfect body would have to be surgically cut, but I also wanted to know the cause of death, simply to know I had not done anything wrong.

I did not know how to process the things that had happened prior to Jasmyn's death, with Dad's sense of her impending death and my urge to pray for her the week she died. I put all this in the back of my mind, not yet ready to consider it.

After the coroner's examination we proceeded with a funeral to celebrate Jasmyn's life. I had a very real sense of Jesus' comfort at the funeral. My sister Robyn and her children, Bethany, Katrina and Matthew, did a great job in helping with the music. We had been preparing to have Jasmyn dedicated to the Lord at church as she was nearly four months old. I talked with Pastor Peter about it and we decided to include the dedication of Jasmyn's life into the first part of the funeral service. That was really beautiful. There was only one thing that made me cry. That was when, at the end of the service, Pastor Peter asked Leigh to come forward and carry Jasmyn out in the coffin. Leigh was so strong and I felt overwhelmingly proud of him. He told me afterwards that he did not feel alone, he had Jasmyn with him. For the funeral I wrote a Eulogy of Jasmyn's life which Inge read for us. Let me share it with you as our tribute to Jasmyn.

Jasmyn Evelyn Scott – Eulogy

I was known before I was conceived and I was completely loved and adored. I was knit together in my mother's womb by the hand of God for nine beautiful months. I truly was fearfully and wonderfully made. I was encompassed by peace, love and joy. I had such contentment in my spirit as I grew. I got excited as I started to be able to hear the sounds of my daddy, mummy and my big sister Kirilee. Kirilee would give me pats and chatter away to me. What a delight it was for me to be born, so that I might meet all those who loved me and see them face to face.

That day came on the 13th of October 2005. It was my grandparents, Mac and Maisie's, wedding anniversary. My doctor and daddy were telling so many funny stories to each other that Mummy actually laughed and my head came out! Laughter was the first sounds I heard. What a great and wonderful day my birth was. Mummy and Daddy just loved me so much. I was named Jasmyn because I was as a beautiful, fragrant flower. I was named Evelyn after my Grandma, Joan Evelyn Hicks, and my Great Grandma, Phyllis Evelyn Cronin.

I returned from the hospital in Sydney to see my earthly home for the first time. What a beautiful place to live. Then I met my dear sister Kirilee. How we loved each other. I met Grandma and Grandad and Nan and so many others that came to love me.

Mummy and Daddy cared for me so well. My every need was met and I lived the whole of my life in blissful love and joy. What more could I have wanted? The four of us had such happy family times together. We went for picnics to the river, we fed the ducks, we went swimming at the pool. To celebrate Christmas we went to Carols by Candlelight at Bathurst. We drove around Bathurst to see the Christmas lights. I spent Christmas Eve at Grandma and Grandad's and Christmas Day at Nan's. I was given a lovely swing for Christmas, which I had lots of enjoyment from. We went to church every Sunday and Mummy always dressed me so beautifully. I loved to come to God's house and be surrounded by worship to my God. Mummy read me stories from the Bible nearly every day. I loved listening to music.

When I was three weeks old Daddy babysat me for a few hours while Mummy went out. Mummy gave Daddy instructions to put me to bed by 8.45 pm. When Mummy came home an hour later she was shocked to find me still up playing with Daddy. But I had been such a good girl and was having so much fun with Daddy he just kept me up. I had the best Daddy in the world and we just loved being together.

Kirilee was my best little friend. Every day as I had my feeds she would come up to my head and kiss me. Then she would say "More" and kiss me again and again. When we would go riding in the pram together she would just reach out and hold my hand. If Kirilee heard me crying, she would always tell Mummy to make sure I was OK. I loved Kirilee so much and I know she loved me. Only two weeks ago we had our first tea party at Grandma's. We had so much fun together.

My last day on this earth came sooner than anyone expected. It was last Friday, 3 February 2006. I was at my grandma and grandad's. Mummy was there and I spent my last time with her talking, cuddling, kissing and playing. I lay on the floor with her and was rolling around, laughing at my toy Humpty. Mummy put me to bed and I woke up in heaven! I didn't suffer. My life on earth was complete. Now I am with my Maker, the one who gave me to Mummy and Daddy in the first place. I am with my best friend Jesus. I am also with my older brother and sister, Jack and Lily, and how wonderful it is to have them with me. We will have a lot of fun together.

I had a perfect life. It was short, but it was perfect. Every moment was so wonderful. Thank you so much to everyone who loved me and cared for me. My life is not finished, but only just begun. I am waiting in heaven to see you again, where my joy and yours will be complete. I love you with all my heart, Daddy, Mummy and Kirilee – until we meet again...

Your beloved Jasmyn

Chapter 13

RESTORATION

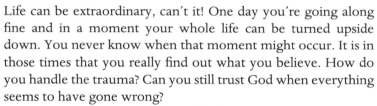

Life can be extraordinary, can't it! One day you're going along fine and in a moment your whole life can be turned upside down. You never know when that moment might occur. It is in those times that you really find out what you believe. How do you handle the trauma? Can you still trust God when everything seems to have gone wrong?

In the midst of the shock, grief and pain, I still did trust God. A friend of mine asked me if Jasmyn dying made me doubt God. I told her that God had proved Himself to me over so many years. Instead of blaming God and turning away from Him, I turned to Him, needing Him more than ever to help me come through this crisis. Each part of the journey that I have already described was like a brick in my foundation, Jesus was my cornerstone. In Matthew 7:24-25 Jesus has this to say about a wise man,

> "Therefore everyone who hears these words of mine and puts them into practice is like a wise man who built his house on the rock. The rain came down, the streams rose, and the winds blew and beat against that house; yet it did not fall, because it had its foundation on the rock."

I was certainly in the midst of a violent storm, but amazingly I did have a peace and an inner strength that could only come from God.

I also told my friend that I knew even in the midst of that storm that God would bring good out of Jasmyn's life. I was expectant of the good fruit that would be manifest in five, ten and twenty years' time. I could not see the good at the time or imagine what it might be, but I was confident in the character of God. Paul says in Romans 8:28:

> And we know that in all things God works for the good of those who love him, who have been called according to his purpose.

I knew God would work Jasmyn's life and death for good. Notwithstanding my trust in God, never before had I known such pain and grief as I went through in those early weeks after Jasmyn left us. For me it felt like the swell of a huge ocean wave coming upon me. The emotion, pain and grief would rise within me and I would cry like I had never cried before. When the tears were spent I would be exhausted and very flat emotionally. The wave would pass. I never knew how long it would be or where I would be when it came again.

So many people – family and friends – were incredibly kind to us, helping us with meals, doing any jobs we asked for help with, blessing us in unexpected ways. I knew we were in the midst of a major crisis. People could certainly come "unstuck" by something like this and never get over it. I determined that it was not going to happen to us. I recognized also that I needed God to give us a plan to help us in the process of healing.

The first thing I did was plan a week's holiday at the beach for early in March. That helped me in the weeks leading up to it because it gave me something to look forward to. I knew that Leigh needed to get away and it would be really good for us to have time together as a family. We needed to keep our hope alive. I also knew that I needed to have some counseling, and so I spoke with Diane Watson at Ellel Gilbulla and arranged a prayer ministry appointment for the week we were on holiday.

The Coroner's Report confirmed that Jasmyn's death was a case of Sudden Infant Death Syndrome (SIDS), formerly known as cot death. That did help. The thing that I was finding most difficult to process was that Jasmyn had been so happy, content and healthy, and then she was gone. She had never even had a cold or any kind of sickness. It just did not seem right.

I took every day as it came. I was not hard on myself and if I needed to cry, then I gave myself permission. One of the hardest things in the early weeks was the feeling of empty hands. When I went to do the washing there were only half the clothes there to be done. I really missed being able to "do" something. I did not have so much to "do" now.

One of the greatest pains I felt was for Kirilee who had lost her sister. Kirilee was sixteen and a half months old when Jasmyn died. Many say that children do not understand, but I was amazed by her perception. We told her that Jasmyn had gone to sleep. She would go into Jasmyn's bedroom, pat the cradle and say "night night." That always made me want to cry. But I had to facilitate Kirilee's grieving also.

Leigh and I grieved completely differently. It was really hard to help each other when we were both hurting so much. Leigh did not ever really bring me the comfort I needed – to expect him to do so would have been unfair. I had to give him the space to grieve in his own way, and he had to let me grieve in my own way. The comfort I needed could be found only in the person of Jesus. So to Him I brought my heart.

In his Sermon on the Mount Jesus says: "Blessed are those who mourn, for they will be comforted" (Matthew 5:4). I needed His touch and He gave it to me. I had grace for every day. I was thankful for all the blessings I did have, no longer taking any blessing for granted.

The time arrived for our holiday at the beach. We took Mum with us. She was still pained by the whole experience, having found Jasmyn with me, and she also felt a sense of responsibility that Jasmyn had died in her home, although it was clearly not her burden to carry. We needed to relax, rest and try to have some fun, for Kirilee's sake as well as for our own. We took her to the beach and played with her in the rock pools. On one occasion, as I looked at her playing in the sand, I felt such pain for her. She was supposed to have a little sister there with her, but she was all alone.

I went to visit Ellel Gilbulla for my personal ministry appointment. Diane and another counselor were there waiting for me. What a blessing. The ministry we had that day was foundational to my walking through the journey ahead back into wholeness. We talked about the grief and the feelings of anger I was experiencing – even the feeling of anger with God for letting Jasmyn die. I had to forgive myself and have the burden of responsibility and guilt lifted off me that in some way Jasmyn's death had been my fault.

The most difficult but most powerful part of the ministry that day was when we prayed for Jesus to come and sever the soul-tie between me and Jasmyn. As with Jack and Lily, Jasmyn was gone. Holding onto her was not going to serve any further good purpose. I had to trust her back to Jesus. One beautiful thing that the Holy Spirit showed me was that Jasmyn was being cared for by the King of Kings (Isaiah 49:23a).

Then Diane prayed that Leigh and I would have another child. We prayed about the fear and anxiety which I knew would be near if we had another child. I left Ellel feeling lighter, as if a heavy load had been lifted from me.

For the remainder of our holiday I wanted to hear from God, and each day I would walk up to a nearby bluff looking over the ocean waves beating against the coastline and pray. One of the days I felt Jesus' sweet presence and His word came to me again. We had had four children: three were in heaven and only one was with us on earth. I was believing God to restore to us what had been lost. He took me again to the story of Abraham, specifically to the part where Abraham was tested by God and presented Isaac his son as an offering to God (Genesis 22:1-18). When Abraham brought Isaac as an offering he believed that God could raise the dead and "he did receive Isaac back from death" (Hebrews 11:19). I was telling God how I had laid down my daughter Jasmyn and that I trusted Him to bring her "back from death." He encouraged me to read the story again. The basis of that story is Abraham's *son*. The Holy Spirit showed me that He was speaking to me about our son Jack, whom I had given to Him. He promised me that He would give us a son, because I had believed God as Abraham had done and He credited it to me as righteousness. I was going to receive my son back from the dead (Hebrews 11:35)!

As a confirmation of this promise God gave me a second scripture. Some years before God had spoken to me from Ecclesiastes 11:1:

> "Cast your bread upon the waters, for after many days you will find it again."

I had never fully understood why He had spoken that to me or what it meant. That day, looking out over the ocean, I understood. My "bread" was my children. They were a part of my body. I had indeed cast them on the water. I looked far out to the horizon and saw a sailing boat way out at sea heading towards the shore. Jesus said to me, "Your son is coming"! Jesus was promising to return to me that which I had given to Him!
I asked if He had a name for this son. He told me that our son's name was to be Izaak! I walked down from the bluff with great excitement in my heart. But I knew I was going into the hardest part – the time between the promise being given and the promise being fulfilled.

That month I became pregnant again. I prayed for God's grace upon our new baby, knowing I was still grieving, not wanting any feelings of grief, fear or rejection to be felt by the baby. I know I was doing the best I could and facing a new pregnancy after all that we had been through was nothing short of courageous. Satan would whisper in my ear, "What if you have another miscarriage?" and "What if you make it through the pregnancy and then the baby dies of a cot death like Jasmyn?" It is one of Satan's favorite tactics to try to undermine God and try to make you doubt as he did in the Garden of Eden with Eve (see Genesis 3:1). Being still so vulnerable, the fear was very real to me. What if those things did happen? I knew I could not handle another loss like the loss of Jasmyn. I had put my trust entirely in God and if this did not work out, I would be sunk.

I asked God for a promise for this baby that I could hold on to. When I was about three months into the pregnancy God gave it to me. Driving along in the car, I put on a CD of a man speaking out different Bible passages. All of a sudden one particular scripture jumped off the CD, and I felt it touch my heart and then amazingly move into my little baby. The promise was for us both. It was the promise God gave to Gideon: "Peace! Do not be afraid. You are not going to die" (Judges 6:23)! I was so touched. That was exactly the word I needed. It very bluntly told me I was not to be afraid of the baby dying and to be at peace. So I started praying the promise and declaring it over our baby every day.

One other Scripture that God used to really speak to me was my favorite Psalm 23. Living on a farm, the picture of the Lord being our Shepherd spoke powerfully to me. In his early years Leigh had tended sheep and, in the same way as he had watched over a ewe expecting a lamb, the Lord was going to watch over me, providing me with protection and safety. The Lord showed me that He was going to meet every one of my needs as I walked through pregnancy. This assurance provided me with a great sense of security.

There were a few things that I did in the early months that helped me as I grieved. At Jasmyn's burial some of our family had arranged for some helium balloons, which were released into the sky near the end of the ceremony. The symbolism of the balloons was very powerful to me, making me think of Jasmyn's soul having been taken from her body on earth and transported by angels to heaven. Knowing there are no rules about grieving, I decided to use balloons to help me. In the early weeks and months, if there was ever a time I particularly wanted to release a feeling or thought to Jasmyn, I would buy a balloon and we would write on it with a texta. I would say whatever it was that I wanted to say, Kirilee would draw on it and Leigh would also write on it. Then we would kiss it and release it together, watching it float way up into the sky until we could see it no more. Sometimes we would go to the cemetery to do it, other times we would release it from home. It was a means by which we could all express and release our feelings. Ever since that time we have bought balloons for Jasmyn's birthday and for the anniversary of her death. For our family it is now a special part of remembering Jasmyn and a way in which we can celebrate her life.

Before Jasmyn died, we had been planning to go to the Sydney Royal Easter Show in March that year. Leigh had recently started showing cattle in the big agricultural show, and since he had already entered one of the steers, we decided we would still go. I felt the pain of Jasmyn's absence, knowing we had planned for her to be there with us. So we bought a beautiful, huge helium balloon in the shape of a butterfly and again we all wrote on it, kissed it and released it to her from the showground. I had peace then. Leigh's steer won too, which made it exciting for us.

I also spent time reading and searching the Scriptures for passages that related to the loss of children. One of the passages that brought me great comfort was from Matthew 18, where Jesus, having been asked who is the greatest in the kingdom of heaven, speaks of the value of children. In verse 10 of that chapter Jesus makes this amazing statement,

> "See that you do not look down on one of these little ones. For I tell you that their angels in heaven always see the face of my Father in heaven."

Jack, Lily and Jasmyn were being cared for by angels, who always see the face of the Father! I found that so comforting.

Another scripture that really touched me comes from the mouth of a godly man called Job who had seven sons and three daughters. However, Satan brings his hand against Job and all his children are killed – I thought losing three children was bad, but Job lost ten all at once! Listen to what Job says in worship to God when he hears the news:

> "Naked I came from my mother's womb,
> and naked I shall depart.
> The Lord gave and the Lord has taken away;
> may the name of the Lord be praised."

(Job 1:21)

To me, being able to speak these words when he has just lost
all his children, is such an amazing illustration of faith and trust
in God.

I was also deeply helped by a book a friend had given Mum
for me at Jasmyn's funeral. It was called *Eternity: The Vision of
Marietta Davis* (rewritten by Dennis and Nolene Prince, RCM
Publications, 2000), and was based on a heavenly vision that a
young lady named Marietta Davis had in 1848. I found the parts of
the vision where Marietta talks about babies in heaven extremely
touching and God used it to minister to me very deeply in the
early months after Jasmyn died. While the book must be taken
for what it is – a retelling of a vision and not Scripture – I would
recommend it to anyone who has lost a young child or baby in
whatever circumstances.

Another special thing I did which was a great help to me, was
I picked out all my favorite photos of Jasmyn and put together a
collage, which I had framed by a local picture framer. I wanted
to keep it as a lasting legacy of Jasmyn's life. When Jasmyn died I
had also been given a photo book, which I decided to use to dis-
play all the photographs of Kirilee and Jasmyn together. I wrote
stories with each photograph and have kept it for Kirilee as a
special book to remember her little sister.

At our church there was a beautiful older lady named Margaret
Gittoes, who had taken a special interest in first Kirilee and then
Jasmyn, always having a little talk to them and giving Kirilee the
odd little gift. Unbeknown to me, Margaret was an artist. When
Jasmyn died she talked to Mum about the possibility of her doing
a painting of Jasmyn for us and Mum secretly arranged for her to
have a photograph to work with. Some time later, one Sunday
morning Margaret sidled up to me with a gift wrapped up in a
paper bag. When I opened it I was totally blown away: it was the
most beautiful framed portrait of Jasmyn lying on her side. The
colors were perfect. Margaret had used her gift to bless us and be
a part of God's bigger picture of healing. Think how wonderful
it would be if lots more people used their gifts, whatever they
might be, to bless people who were having a really hard time!
Margaret's painting will remain in the living room of our home
forever, bringing us a gentle reminder of Jasmyn. Margaret

passed away last year after a short illness and I wanted to honor her by telling what she did. I know she will be in heaven playing with Jasmyn even now.

I progressed through the pregnancy, going through all the things I had gone through with Kirilee and Jasmyn. When I came to the nineteen-week ultrasound I decided to go alone. I knew I was going to find out if the baby was a boy or a girl and I needed some space to process it. I would be happy either way, but I knew it would be emotional. The baby was again a beautiful girl! Emotionally that was probably more difficult for me, but I trusted that God knew what He was doing and that He had a higher plan. At least we had been given the opportunity to have another child, which some families in the same position are not given.

The ultrasound also showed that my placenta was very low in my womb, which caused a potential for significant complications as the pregnancy progressed. The main threat was bleeding and a premature delivery. I had little choice again but to ask God to hold me in the palm of His hand. I could not handle complications. We had lots of people praying for us, including our family and church, Peter Horrobin and many from Ellel Ministries, which meant a great deal to us.

Amazingly I went through the entire pregnancy without losing a drop of blood. However, since there had been no change in the position of my placenta, at thirty-nine weeks Dr Bell admitted me to hospital in Sydney for a compulsory Caesarean delivery. Our beautiful new princess was born – Laura Jasmyn Scott, weighing 9 pounds 2 ounces! Leigh cut her umbilical cord. My favorite memory of the birth is that, when she was born in the operating theater, she was crying as babies do, so the nurse brought her around to me near my face and as soon as she heard my voice talking to her she stopped crying. She knew me! I thought that was beautiful. I also loved her cute blond hair. It was all so amazing. Laura was born on the 12th of December 2006, just in time for Christmas!

We had done it. God had been faithful again. Now we had to face the first year of Laura's life and continue to walk in our healing, trusting God in everything.

Chapter 14

TO RECEIVE A DOUBLE PORTION

—————————— ≈ ——————————

Laura's birth brought us immense joy and comfort, but it also stirred some fear and anxiety. Once we got through the first year I knew it would become easier. Strangely, the thing I was most afraid of was the sound of silence. I wanted to live by faith and not be neurotically checking Laura many times while she was asleep. Every day, week and month was a victory. I had to trust God to watch over Laura every time I put her to bed.

When we reached the two-month mark, I went through a difficult time. Between two and four months is the most common time for babies to die from SIDS. It also coincided with the anniversary of Jasmyn's death the year before. I could feel a wave of depression coming over me. I kept on wanting to cry. I cried out to God again for His special grace to help me through.

I could have gone to get professional help, but I hoped that with the right support and with prayer I could get through it. The first thing I knew I had to do was admit I had a problem. Then I had to put together a plan to get through it. I talked to my family and to Inge about how I was feeling, and they were praying for me. Then I went to talk to Pastor Peter at church. I told him I could feel the depression trying to come upon me, and that I did not want to take it on. I asked if he could allocate someone at church to pray especially for me for the remainder of

Laura's first year. We agreed together to ask Margaret, the lady who had painted Jasmyn's portrait for us. So Margaret supported me in prayer especially through that year and it made all the difference. I did not become depressed or need any treatment. The local church can be such a blessing!

Every day as I put Laura to bed I would pray over her the promise that God had given me, saying, "Peace be with you, Laura. Do not be afraid: you will not die but you will live and declare the praises of the Lord." God's promises also make the world of difference.

During the middle of that year God started to speak to me again from the book of Job. Job trusted God despite all the many difficulties he experienced in his life and, near the end of his life, God gave him a double portion for all he had lost (Job 42:10). Not only did God give him double the number of animals he had owned in the first place, but for every son he had lost, God gave him a son and for every daughter God gave him a daughter – seven sons and three daughters (Job 42:13)! How is that a double portion? Because the sons and daughters in heaven count in the inheritance! Do you see? My miscarried babies Jack and Lily and our daughter Jasmyn really mattered to God. They will be a part of my inheritance when I get to heaven. What God was promising me was a son for my son and a daughter for each of my daughters! I had one son and two daughters in heaven. He was saying He was going to give me a son and two daughters on earth! Wow! God had given me Kirilee for Lily and Laura for Jasmyn, and He was now promising me a son for Jack! These scriptures became my life and my hope. This promise also tied in with the other promises He had spoken to me about having a son, the first one going back to when Jasmyn was conceived.

During one Sunday morning service Pastor Peter announced that there was a one-day regional women's conference coming up on the theme of "Born for Such a Time as This." Although I had never gone to any of the other regional women's conferences, as soon as I saw the flyer for this one I knew I should go. God stirred something in my spirit, and when that happens I have learnt it is best to respond to His leading.

It was not easy for me to get away. The conference was in a city named Dubbo, a three-hour drive from our home. Laura was ten months old by then and I had to arrange for Mum to mind her for the day. But from the moment I walked in the door of the church, I knew it was my day and God had something special for me. I wanted God to confirm to me that He was going to give us a double portion and indeed a son. At the beginning of the first session the pastor had two gifts to give out: the first to the lady who had been the last to register – that was me! – and the second to the lady who had come from the furthest away – that was me too! I had never before won any prizes and here I was winning both of the ones on offer.

The guest speaker at the conference was a lady named Pastor Fran Gullo. I enjoyed the day's teaching and meeting ladies from other churches. Near the end of the conference Pastor Fran offered to pray for people. I knew that this was why I was here. When Pastor Fran came over to pray for me, I told her I believed that God had promised me we would have a son, and I briefly told her my story. I also told her some of the scriptures God had been giving me, one of which was, "many who are first will be last, and the last first" (Mark 10:31). I believed that through this scripture God was saying that Jack my son had been my first child, but He was going to return a son to us as our last child. As I shared this with Pastor Fran she recalled how I had been the last to register and that she had been going to say to me right at the beginning of the morning, "The last shall be first." This was a confirmation of God's promise. Both from Pastor Fran's teaching and our ministry time together God gave me another most amazing confirmation.

> Instead of their shame my people will receive a double
> portion, and instead of disgrace they will rejoice in their
> inheritance; and so they will inherit a double portion in
> their land, and everlasting joy will be theirs.
>
> (Isaiah 61:7)

I also felt the double gifts in the morning was another confirmation of God promising us a double portion.

When I arrived home that night I was buzzing with excitement. God had confirmed the promise of a double portion to me from an external source. Whenever I think I have received a word or a promise from God, I always like to test it in case it was just my good idea. I always ask God to confirm His promises to me from external sources so I can be really sure. He had done it again. The double portion promise was not just my good idea! It was really God.

Laura turned one in December, and that was such a thrill for me. We had all made it through the year. God had again proved Himself faithful. Laura was such a delight to me and I was so grateful to God for the wonderful gift of both Kirilee and Laura. As all parents would understand, your children touch your heart in a way you could never have imagined until you experience it. Given also what we had lost, I appreciated them so much more. The joy and the pride I experienced as they started to crawl and talk and walk is incomparable to any other emotion I have ever felt.

I had always fallen pregnant very easily. Once Laura was one I felt ready to try one more time for our son. But God made me wait. Through that time of waiting I held the promises in my heart and I prayed as I have never prayed before. My child-bearing season was coming to an end. A doctor once told me that the probability of my having a son when I had had four pregnancies in a row bearing daughters, was low. However, I put my faith, hope and trust in God, believing He would be faithful to His promises to me.

In September 2008, to my great excitement, I fell pregnant again. I knew this was it. We went to Dr Bell again. My nineteen-week ultrasound showed that the placenta was low as it had been in Laura's pregnancy, but partly covering the cervix as well this time. I was again at high risk of complications, including hemor-rhaging and premature delivery, especially because this was my sixth pregnancy and one of my previous deliveries had been by Caesarean section, not to mention my advancing age!

I let God hold me in the palm of His hand and, thankfully, the weeks gradually whittled away. We were again supported in prayer by my family, our new church (C3 Church Bathurst), Peter Horrobin and Ellel Ministries. Due to my high risk factors

Dr Bell decided he was going to admit me into hospital just after thirty-seven weeks to rest, planning delivery for thirty-nine weeks. As Leigh drove me in the car to Sydney I breathed a sigh of relief, knowing that everything was going to be all right. I had made it to full term and I was going to be at the hospital from there on. Leigh was going to see me to the hospital, stay the night and go home the next morning.

It was a Tuesday afternoon when I arrived at the hospital. Leigh stayed at the hospital with me that night. As I was trying to rest, at around 4.30 am I felt a bit damp and asked him to go into our adjoining toilet and get some toilet paper. He rolled over the other way and told me – as only a man would – to go back to sleep, everything would be all right! Only after me insisting did he reluctantly get up to discover that my waters had spontaneously broken! We rang for the midwife. My two-week rest had lasted fifteen hours and I was very suddenly getting ready for an emergency Caesarean delivery! Dr Bell and all the midwives were amazed at the timing of my admission to hospital. I was so thrilled that Leigh was still there with me as he had been going to go home after breakfast.

At 7.52 am on 20 May 2009 our son was born – Izaak Charles Leigh Scott!!! He weighed 7 pounds and 11 ounces. Izaak was born the day before Leigh's mother Maisie's birthday and two days before Leigh's birthday! God's timing is just perfect! We did indeed receive our double portion blessing from God and we named him Izaak in honor of Him. When Abraham and Sarah had Isaac in Genesis 21:6, "Sarah said, 'God has brought me laughter, and everyone who hears about this will laugh with me.'" So it is with us!

Chapter 15

TRUSTING JESUS

It has been a privilege to share my story with you. I am sure that you have been amazed with me as you have seen God's hand at work in my life. There were certainly some bends in the road that none of us expected.

Maybe you have never known Jesus as your Lord and Savior, but after reading this story you want Him to be a part of your life. Or maybe you already know Jesus, but have been challenged to consecrate your life to Him in a deeper way. Either way I want to invite you to share this prayer with me:

Lord Jesus, I acknowledge my need of You and accept You as my Savior.

I invite You now to be Lord of my life,
Lord of my spirit and my relationship with You,
Lord of my body and my behavior,
Lord of my mind and my thinking,
Lord of my emotions and my reactions,
Lord of my will and all of my decisions,
Lord of my sexuality,
Lord of my time, my home, my family, my possessions and
    all of my relationships with others,
Thank You that Your blood was shed that
    I might be free. Amen.

(Ellel Ministries' Lordship Prayer)

The best decision I have ever made was to pray a prayer like this, many years ago now. I have come to know Jesus and He is the most wonderful, faithful and loving friend. When I think back to how God spoke to me at that conference in 1993 and said, "I have heard the cry of your heart and I am going to show you how much I love you," I believe that was not only a word for me: I believe it is also God's word for you! Allow it to touch your heart right now.

Since God spoke that word to me, I have walked an extraordinary journey. It has been far from easy, with great suffering and heartache. I fell off a cliff and went through two and a half years of pain and suffering. I went through many years of loneliness while I was single, wondering if God would bring me a husband. I went through the loss of three children, two by miscarriage and one from SIDS. I have lived in and walked through the valley of death. But look at the amazing works God has done through my suffering! I was miraculously physically, emotionally and spiritually healed from the effects of the accident, before a very amazed crowd of doctors, health professionals and pastors! I have walked in that freedom ever since. I have had minor health issues from time to time, but nothing that has ever stopped me from living my life to the full. I managed six pregnancies in just under seven years and am now a full-time mum – the most demanding job I have ever done. I was given the honor by God to be the seed by which Ellel Ministries was birthed in Australia, bringing God's love, healing and restoration to so many in Australia and in surrounding nations. As I put God first in my life, He gave me the abounding joy of bringing me my heart's desire. God gave me the most beautiful love story with the most wonderful man, my darling Leigh, who loved me and wanted to marry me from the moment we met. He blessed us with a home and farm that is so beautiful. God has given us a double portion blessing, giving us a child for each child we lost, son for son and daughter for daughter. His hand was clearly upon each one of our children and their births, Kirilee even being born on the eighth anniversary of my healing! You may wonder if I have ever regretted trusting the Lord – **no, never!** God has been 100 per cent faithful to every single promise He gave me and blessed me in ways I could never have dreamed of.

I referred to two incidents before the accident, one where God asked me if I would trust Him with my life, even if it included physical suffering, and the other where He supernaturally came upon my body and strengthened it eight days before the accident. I also referred to a few incidents before Jasmyn died, which led to a sense that something might happen to her. I did not understand it at the time, but in hindsight it is now clearer. God was preparing Jasmyn to go to heaven. People may say, "Do you mean that God caused the accident?" or "Do you mean God caused Jasmyn to die?" Christians also have a tendency to say things like "God must have allowed it." Let me be very clear: I believe these are the wrong questions to ask. These questions are based on doubt and blame, seeking to doubt the love, power and goodness of God and/or to shift the blame of an incident that is difficult to reconcile on to God. The question is not "Did God cause it?" or "Did God allow it?" The question is: **"When difficult things come your way, will you trust Him?"** The Bible demonstrates the trustworthiness of God and my story demonstrates the trustworthiness of God. The gospel of Jesus Christ does work. Undoubtedly we all sooner or later face difficulties of different kinds. If you will trust God in the midst of your suffering He will bring miracles out of your difficulties that you never could have imagined. Even when your emotions are screaming at you in pain, trust Jesus, as I did. He will come through for you as He did for me.

Some may say that a loving God would not ask you to go through physical suffering. God asked me if I would trust Him. God may not ask everyone to go through physical suffering, but He asks each of us to trust Him and our response to Him is critical. Jesus trusted the Father and knew that He was going to endure physical suffering. Like anyone in the face of physical pain and death Jesus cried out,

"Father, if you are willing, take this cup from me; yet not my will, but yours be done."

(Luke 22:42)

The next verse tells us that "An angel from heaven appeared to him and strengthened him." I had trusted Jesus, wanting only His will in my life, and maybe it was an angel that strengthened me. Just because we may have to go through some very painful suffering does not mean that God does not love us or that He has abandoned us. Jesus never doubted the Father's love in the face of suffering and nor should we. Look at the glory given to Jesus for the suffering He went through. For the joy set before Him, Jesus endured the cross, scorning its shame and is now seated at the right hand of the throne of God (Hebrews 12:2)! Countless billions of people throughout the centuries have come into relationship with the Father through Jesus. But He had to die on a cross.

God was not having a sleep when I fell off the cliff and woke up with a shock to discover what had happened! God was not looking the other way when Jack, Lily and Jasmyn died and then thought He had better come up with some way to make it up to us. God was right there with us through it all, even when we could not see Him or hear Him. Most likely He was carrying us in His arms of love, holding us near His heart. Why did He let it happen? Sometimes there are no answers and we have to be content with that. But as I trusted Him through the pain He was then able to unlock miracles for us and reveal His love in ways that would not have been possible if I had not trusted Him. It took time, commitment and faith. He answered me in ways that were different from my ways, but were ultimately for my good.

Sometimes we also understand suffering in hindsight. In the scheme of things two and a half years of pain and suffering was nothing really compared with the blessing that God had intended to bring out of the accident for the good of so many people. At the time I did not know what God had planned. But now I understand. God wanted to give understanding to the Body of Christ about how to bring healing to victims of accident and trauma. Through Ellel Ministries my story has made an impression on many, many people's lives around the world in the whole area of accident and trauma ministry.

If you have been a victim of a major accident or trauma and still bear the scars, take heart. There is hope for you. Jesus Christ wants to heal you and make you whole, just as He did me. The price has been paid for you to be healed through Jesus. Find your nearest Ellel Center to learn more. Your healing may not be as dramatic and quick as my healing, but if you will reach out to Jesus in your brokenness He will heal and restore you, body, soul and spirit.

So what is our purpose on this earth? I believe it is to live for the glory of God. Jesus brought glory to the Father by completing the work He gave Him to do (John 17:4). As we live our lives in love and obedience to Jesus we show ourselves to be His disciples, and as we complete the work that He has given us to do, we also will bring glory to the Father (John 15:8). This may include suffering as it did with Jesus, but as a result of our suffering glory will come. I hope that my suffering has shown you the glory of God and inspired you to live for His glory also.

As I close, I urge you to determine in your heart today that you will trust Jesus, come what may. I have received some of my rewards from Jesus already and I know more will come as I continue to walk in love, faith and trust in Him. But I also look forward to the time when I leave this earth to go to heaven. My joy will be complete when I get to be in the presence of my best Friend, my Heavenly Father before His throne, when I see Jesus face to face and feel His touch. When that wonderful day comes I know Jesus will take me by the hand and reunite me with Jack, Lily and Jasmyn. What joy will be mine! In the fullness of time I will wait for the other half of our family on earth to be joined with us and our whole family will be together as one for the first time. Then I will live in the fullness of my double portion inheritance for eternity!

> "They overcame him by the blood of the Lamb
> and by the word of their testimony;
> they did not love their lives so much
> as to shrink from death."

(Revelation 12:11)

The Truth & Freedom Series

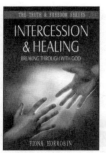

Rescue from Rejection: Finding Security in God's Loving Acceptance
Denise Cross
£7.99 / 160pp

The Dangers of Alternative Ways to Healing: How to Avoid New Age Deceptions
David Cross & John Berry
£8.99 / 176pp

Intercession & Healing: Breaking Through with God
Fiona Horrobin
£7.99 / 176pp

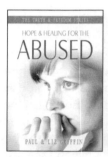

Hope & Healing for the Abused
Paul & Liz Griffin
£6.99 / 128pp

Trapped by Control: How To Find Freedom
David Cross
£6.99 / 112pp

Anger: How Do You Handle It?
Paul & Liz Griffin
£6.99 / 112pp

Sex: God's Truth
Jill Southern
£6.99 / 128pp

Soul Ties: The Unseen Bond in Relationships
David Cross
£6.99 / 128pp

God's Covering: A Place of Healing
David Cross
£7.99 / 192pp

**Available from all good Christian bookshops.
For more information about these titles visit:**

www.sovereignworld.com

Recommended Titles

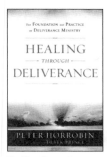

**Healing through
Deliverance (hardback)**
Peter Horrobin
£24.99 / 586pp

**Living the Life (FREE DVD)
Breaking through with God**
Peter Horrobin
£9.99 / 224pp

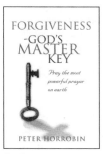

**Forgiveness –
God's Master Key**
Peter Horrobin
£6.99 / 112pp

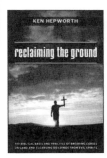

Reclaiming the Ground
Ken Hepworth
£6.99 / 128pp

Pills for the Soul?
Dieter Mulitze
£11.99 / 320pp

Releasing Heaven on Earth
Alistair Petrie
£9.99 / 272pp

Sarah
Sarah Shaw
£8.99 / 176pp

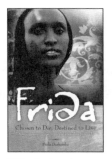

**Frida: A miraculous escape
from the Rwandan genocide**
Frida Gashumba
£8.99 / 176pp

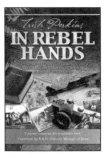

In Rebel Hands
Trish Perkins
£12.99 / 416pp

**Available from all good Christian bookshops.
For more information about these titles visit:**

www.sovereignworld.com

We hope you enjoyed reading this
Sovereign World book.
For more details of other Sovereign
books and new releases see our website:

www.sovereignworld.com

You can also join us on Facebook and Twitter.

To promote this title kindly consider writing
a review on our Facebook page, shelfari.com, Amazon,
or for posting to any online retailer.

If you would like to help us send a copy of
this book and many other titles to needy
pastors in developing countries, please
write for further information or send
your gift to:

Sovereign World Trust
PO Box 777
Tonbridge
Kent
TN11 0ZS
United Kingdom

www.sovereignworldtrust.org.uk

The Sovereign World Trust
is a registered charity.